LONG AND WINDING ROAD

THE **GREATEST** **BEATLES** **STORIES** **EVER** TOLD

Edited by Luis Miguel

FanReads
Toronto, Canada

www.fanreads.com

First Edition

ISBN 978-1-988420-07-3 (paperback)
ISBN 978-1-988420-06-6 (electronic)

Cover by Inspired Cover Design
Book design by Keith McArthur

Printed and bound in the United States of America.

FanReads Inc.
Suite #912
6A The Donway West
Toronto, Ontario M3C 2E8

www.fanfeads.com
contact@fanreads.com

To my wife, Silvia; and to my daughters,
Leah and Zahra.

Contents

[Introduction]

By Luis Miguel

W hen I was between eighth and ninth grade, my family moved from California to Georgia. Knowing no one and having nothing to do other than explore the woods behind our house, I decided one day to rummage through the many assorted CDs my uncle had give us upon our arrival to the Peach State.

What caught my attention about the diverse collection was the inclusion of all thirteen Beatles albums (including *Yellow Submarine* and *Magical Mystery Tour*).

I'd heard of the Beatles before, but really knew nothing about them except that one of their members, a guy named Paul McCartney, had sung a duet with Michael Jackson on *Thriller*.

After Googling the Beatles and reading about how influential they were, I decided to give them a shot. I would listen to each of their albums in the order they were released.

So I put *Please Please Me* into the CD player and hit play . . .

I'm sure you can guess the rest of the story. If you're reading this, it's probably because at some point you had your own very personal first experience with the Beatles.

And what is it about the Beatles' music that makes its discovery such a transformative life event? Why are we still talking and listening, reading and writing about them after a half century?

It's more than their cultural influence. It's more than the advances in recording and the unprecedented sales figures. Those are all secondary.

What makes the Beatles great—what makes them as relevant to kids today as the young baby boomers growing up in the 60s—is that John, Paul, George, and Ringo speak to you personally through their music. They manage to put lyrics to the feelings, the conflicts, the joys, and the heartbreaks we all go through. *Their* words become *our* words.

Whether it's the awkward insecurity expressed in "I Want to Tell You," the emotionally burned out fatigue of "I'm So Tired," or the powerful spiritual reassurance of "Let it Be," you can't help thinking that the Beatles know what you're feeling. They've been where you are and understand what you're going through. And that brings peace. It's as though you have four friends always at your side.

This book isn't so much about relating all the details of the Beatles' history—there are many great books that do that already—as it is about creating an impression. That in the time you spend reading it you feel as though you're meeting again with those four old friends you hadn't seen in a while.

Long and Winding Road follows the Beatles' story in a loose chronological fashion. There are words from the Fab Four themselves describing their rocky journey to greatness, with the anticipated misadventures—including Paul's description of the time they played backing music in a gentleman's club for one Janice the Stripper.

There are first-hand accounts from people who witnessed the great historic events, such as *The Ed Sullivan Show* appearance and the Shea Stadium performance. There are tales of the motley crew that made up the Beatles wide network of friends: road manager Mal Evans, producer George Martin, actor Peter Sellers. Even famed boxer Muhammad Ali makes an appearance!

Scholars look at the wide-ranging impact of Liverpool's favorite sons, such as their role in making the album the primary artistic medium in popular music. On the lighter side, we hear the curious tale of a dentist who wants to clone John Lennon from a tooth, and perhaps definitively find out the identity of the famous "Hard Day's Night" chord.

Now, you may ask: Why *Long and Winding Road* when there are so many other song titles that could have been re-purposed as book titles? *Long and Winding Road* gets to the heart of why the Beatles matter to us. Life is a journey. By their songs, the Beatles reach out and make us part of their journey. And they become companions to each one of us on our own.

[Timeline]

1940

- July 7: **Ringo Starr** is born (as **Richard Starkey**) at 9 Madryn Street in Dingle, Liverpool.
- October 9: **John Lennon** is born at the Oxford Street Maternity Hospital, Liverpool.

1942

- June 18: **Paul McCartney** is born at the Walton Hospital, Liverpool.

1943

- February 25: **George Harrison** is born in his home at 12 Arnold Grove, Wavertree, Liverpool.

1957

- March: **John Lennon** and school pal **Pete Shotton** start a band, originally called the Black Jacks and later the Quarrymen.
- July 6: Lennon and McCartney meet during an event at the St. Peter's Church garden fête in Liverpool.
- October 18: McCartney's membership with the Quarrymen is made official with his first performance.

1958

- February 6: **George Harrison** joins the band.
- July 15: John's mother **Julia Lennon** is killed by a speeding car.

1960

- May 5: The Quarrymen become the Silver Beetles.
- May 20: **Stu Sutcliffe** begins playing bass for the Silver Beetles.
- August 12: **Pete Best** joins as drummer.
- August 17: The Silver Beetles become the Beatles and begin their first Hamburg residency.
- November 21: Harrison is deported from Germany for being underage.

1961

- March 15: Sutcliffe leaves the group.
- April 1: The Beatles begin their second Hamburg trip.
- June 22: The Beatles are recorded as a backup band for singer **Tony Sheridan**.
- November 9: **Brian Epstein** meets the Beatles. He will go on to become the group's manager.

1962

- January 1: The Beatles audition for Decca. They're ultimately rejected in favor of the Tremeloes.
- April 10: Sutcliffe dies of a brain hemorrhage in Hamburg, Germany.
- May 9: The Beatles are accepted by EMI Producer **George Martin.**
- August 18: **Ringo Starr** is hired to replace Best.

- August 32: Lennon marries **Cynthia Powell**.
- September 4: The Beatles begin recording at Abbey Road Studios.
- October 5: Their "Love Me Do" single is released in the UK.
- October 26: "Love Me Do" Enters the UK charts.

1963

- March 22: UK Release of the *Please Please Me* album.
- November 22: UK Release of *With the Beatles*.
- December 26: UK Release of "I Want to Hold Your Hand" single.

1964

- February 7: The Beatles arrive in New York.
- February 9: The Beatles make their appearance on *The Ed Sullivan Show*.
- July 06: Release of *A Hard Day's Night* film.

1965

- February 11: Starr marries **Maureen Cox**.
- July 29: Release of *Help!* film.
- August 15: The Beatles play at Shea Stadium to a crowd of over 55,000 people.
- December 3: UK Release of *Rubber Soul*.

1966

- January 21: Harrison marries **Pattie Boyd**.
- August 5: UK Release of *Revolver*.
- August 26: Last Beatles concert at Candlestick Park in San Francisco.
- November 9: Lennon meets **Yoko Ono**.

1967

- June 1: Worldwide release of *Sgt. Pepper's Lonely Hearts Club Band.*
- August 27: **Brian Epstein** found dead of a drug overdose in London.
- December 26: Broadcast of the made-for-TV *Magical Mystery Tour* film.

1968

- February 15 & 19: The Beatles travel to the retreat of Indian guru **Maharishi Mahesh Yogi**.
- June 6: Release of *Yellow Submarine* film.
- November 8: John and Cynthia divorce.
- November 22: Worldwide release of *The Beatles* (the White album).

1969

- January 30: The Beatles give their rooftop concert as part of the *Get Back* project.
- March 12: McCartney marries **Linda Eastman**.
- March 20: Lennon marries Yoko Ono.
- September 13: John Lennon plays in Toronto with his Plastic Ono Band—comprised of himself, **Klaus Voorman**, **Eric Clapton**, and **Alan White**.
- September 26: Release of *Abbey Road*.

1970

- April 10: McCartney announces his departure from the Beatles.
- May 8: Release of *Let it Be* album.
- May 13: Release of *Let it Be* film.

- December 31: McCartney files suit to end the Beatles business partnership.

1977

- June 9: Harrison and Pattie Boyd divorce.

1980

- December 8: Lennon is murdered in New York by **Mark David Chapman**.

1994

- December 30: Maureen Cox dies in Seattle, Washington from complications of leukemia.

1995

- November 21: Worldwide release of *Anthology 1*.
- December 4: Worldwide release of *Free as a Bird* single.

1998

April 17: Linda McCartney dies of breast cancer in Tucson.

2001

- November 29: Harrison dies of lung cancer in Los Angeles, California.

2016

- March 8: George Martin dies in his sleep in Wiltshire, England.

[ONE]

The Dubious Origins of the Beatles

By John Lennon

John was a skilled wordplayer with a knack for stream-of-consciousness and free association, as evidenced in the lyrics of songs like Lucy in the Sky with Diamonds and Across the Universe. As early as his school days, John wrote fanciful ditties that he collected in his notebooks. In 1961, Bill Harry of Mersey Beat asked John to write a biography of the Beatles for the magazine. Harry printed John's note without a single edit; we do the same here.
—Luis Miguel

≈

Once upon a time there were three little boys called John, George and Paul, by name christened. They decided to get together because they were the getting together type. When they were together they wondered what for after all, what for? So all of a sudden they grew guitars and fashioned a noise. Funnily enough, no one was interested, least of all the three little men. So-o-o-o on discovering a fourth little even littler man called Stuart Sutcliffe running about them they said, quite 'Sonny get a bass guitar and you will be alright' and he did—but he wasn't alright because he couldn't play it. So they sat on him with comfort 'til he could play. Still there was no beat, and a kindly old man said, quote 'Thou hast not drums!' We had no drums! they coffed. So a series of drums came and went and came.

Suddenly, in Scotland, touring with Johnny Gentle, the group (called the Beatles called) discovered they had not a very nice sound—because they had no amplifiers. They got some.

Many people ask what are Beatles? Why Beatles? Ugh, Beatles, how did the name arrive? So we will tell you. It came in a vision—a man appeared on a flaming pie and said unto them 'From this day on you are Beatles with an 'A'. Thank you, mister man, they said, thanking him.

And then a man with a beard cut off said—will you go to Germany (Hamburg) and play mighty rock for the peasants for money? And we said we would play mighty anything for money.

But before we could go we had to grow a drummer, so we grew one in West Derby in a club called Some Casbah and his trouble was Pete Best. we called 'Hello Pete, come off to Germany!' 'Yes!' Zooooom. After a few months, Peter and Paul (who is called McArtrey, son of Jim McArtrey, his father) lit a Kino (cinema) and the German police said 'Bad Beatles, you must go home and light your English cinemas'. Zooooom, half a group. But before even this, the Gestapo had taken my friend little George Harrison (of speke) away because he was only twelve and too young to vote in Germany; but after two months in England he grew eighteen and the Gestapoes said 'you can come'. So suddenly all back in Liverpool Village were many groups playing in grey suits and Jim said 'Why have you no grey suits?' 'We don't like them, Jim' we said, speaking to Jim.

After playing in the clubs a bit, everyone said 'Go to Germany!' So we are. Zooooom Stuart gone. Zoom zoom John (of Woolton) George (of Speke) Peter and Paul zoom zoom. All of them gone. Thank you club members, from John anf George (what are friends).

∾

"Being a Short Diversion on the Dubious Origins of the Beatles—Translated from the John Lennon," John Lennon. Originally published in Mersey Beat. Copyright Bill Harry.

[TWO]

Origin Story Take Two

By George Harrison

The Beatles would often reflect on the contrast between their humble days of grinding the Liverpool circuit and the madness of non-stop touring/recording cycles. In this message to Mersey Beat, George reminisces fondly on the pre-breakthrough period. —L.M.

∼

I first bought a guitar from a fellow who used to go to junior school with me—Raymond Hughes, and a while later, when I was at Liverpool Institute, I got to know Paul, who lived by me in Speke. I used to travel on the bus with him each morning.

He bought a trumpet—that was a laugh, and we played together at Paul's house—his Dad used to play piano with us, too.

When Paul bought a guitar he found he couldn't play it and sing at the same time.

Paul moved out of Speke but we still kept in contact. He introduced me to John, whose group he joined. At that time I had a skiffle

4

group of my own, but we only played one booking every blue moon and disbanded. Then I joined up with John and Paul. We used to sit at home and play for amusement.

We went on the Liverpool Stadium show on a bill with Gerry, Cass and Rory. By this time Stuart Sutcliffe, a friend of John's from the art college, sold a painting to John Moore and with the money bought a bass and teamed up with us.

We decided to get a drummer to make us into a proper group. Cass got us one, but he was no good. We went to Scotland and came back, but we didn't do much. Pete joined and we went to Hamburg—and the only Shadows number we ever played in Hamburg was 'Apache.' We worked such long hours that we played everything from waltzes to quicksteps, anything we could think of because we were playing for so long.

It's true that we've changed. The differences financially and socially change you in every way. People point at us in the street, and we have no private life—just public life. We're just property, but we like it. We wouldn't do anything else.

∾

"No Private Life But We Love It!" George Harrison. Originally published in Mersey Beat. Copyright Bill Harry.

[THREE]

Original Beatle Stuart Sutcliffe

By Joe Rodgers

Before Lennon/McCartney, there was Lennon/Sutcliffe. Here, Joe Rodgers offers a detailed look at the role of the brilliant artist who served as John's muse and confidant during the Beatles' formative days. The story of the bassist despite himself is worth more than the recollections of wild Hamburg days it provides. John's relationship with Stu Sutcliffe reveals the former's insecurities, sensitivities, and passions in a way that allows for a more profound understanding of Lennon—and, by extension—the Beatles. —L.M.

∾

Otis Redding, Buddy Holly, James Dean, Jim Morrison, Janis Joplin, Brian Jones, Jimi Hendrix, Amy Winehouse, John Bonham, Robert Johnson, Hank Williams, Keith Moon, Kurt Cobain, even Sam Cooke—just many of the musical legends who died young and became instant cultural icons. We have a perverted fascination with those who create a special body of work, then pop their clogs before they get a chance to tarnish their reputation. Many died as a result of depression and/or substance abuse, others simply as a result of being in the wrong place at the wrong time. Stuart Sutcliffe, the original bassist with the Beatles, joined this tragic and iconic club in April 1962.

Sutcliffe's iconic status was assured almost instantly after his death from a cerebral haemorrhage on April 10th 1962. His legend is perpetuated not only by his membership of the most famous group in the history of popular music, particularly during their most uninhibited and formative period, but also by his own independent talent and good looks. His close friendship with one half of the 20th century's most celebrated composing duo, as well as his battles with the other half, have guaranteed that his name is forever inextricably linked to those of Lennon-McCartney and the Beatles. Indeed Sutcliffe receives credit for conceiving the group's name. In addition, the details of his tragic love affair with a beautiful German fiancée who helped to shape the group's early image, and his premature death at the age of 22 make for a fascinating story that writes itself perfectly for a film script . . . and it has.

No fewer than three movies have documented Sutcliffe's life, most famously the 1994 film *BackBeat*. However, as early as 1979, the film *Birth of the Beatles* placed more emphasis on Sutcliffe's character than that of McCartney or Harrison. In addition to these movies, Sutcliffe has been the subject of some four documentaries and at least five books.

Despite this however, his contribution to the Beatles has often been conveniently played down. Sutcliffe was the musically-bereft, James Dean wannabe who was relieved of £65, and selfishly press-ganged into Lennon's group to provide a back-beat on an instrument he couldn't play anyway, right? Well, perhaps on the 50th anniversary of his tragic death, this young man's legacy deserves a second look.

Stuart Victor Ferguson Sutcliffe was born June 22nd 1940 in Edinburgh, Scotland to middle class parents. His father, like John Lennon's, spent the greater part of the war away at sea. The small, effeminate and sensitive Sutcliffe left Grammar school, and with a burgeoning talent for drawing and painting was enrolled at the Liverpool College of Art in 1956 at 16 . . . two years earlier than the average age of enrolment. Moving in Liverpool art school circles, he was introduced to John Lennon sometime in 1957/58 by fellow student Bill Harry, who later founded the paper *Mersey Beat*.

On the surface Lennon and Sutcliffe appeared to be polar opposites. Lennon was already highly skilled at hiding his emotions behind a firewall of aggressive and abusive cruelty towards anyone on his radar. This behaviour moved up a gear at Art College as a defence mechanism to deflect from the fact that he believed himself to be a phony who was in over his head and surrounded by real talent. When it came to applying himself to his studies he was lazy, bored and easily distracted . . . the worst pupil in his class. Sutcliffe on the other hand was gifted with a natural talent for drawing, painting and even sculpture. He was a determined, studious, and meticulous artist who possessed an intensity and dedication which alarmed his tutors. Well aware of the young man's artistic promise, his tutors allowed him to work from his flat although they asked him to slow down and take life easier even then.

Sutcliffe was the most promising student at the college. Cynthia Powell, John Lennon's future wife and art school student, remembers Sutcliffe's nature as being opposite to Lennon's completely. "Stuart was a sensitive artist and he was not a rebel, as John was. He wasn't rowdy or rough" (Mojo, *10 Years That Shook The World* p.26).

Despite their differences however, they possessed a mutual admiration for each other, and for rock 'n' roll. Unlike his jazz influenced art school contemporaries Sutcliffe was influenced by Elvis, which intrigued Lennon, and it was rock 'n' roll's imagery that drew him to Lennon's group.

Lennon was intimidated by Sutcliffe's talent and particularly by his image. Sutcliffe however also admired Lennon's cartoons, particularly their honest and satirical subject matter.

Sutcliffe's praise of his work had the effect of making Lennon feel he actually belonged at the art college. He also fulfilled Lennon's desire to be taken seriously by a serious artist whom he looked up to.

Sutcliffe flattered Lennon and fulfilled an early role as a muse, a role later occupied by Yoko Ono. Indeed Sutcliffe introduced Lennon to *Dadaism*, a movement Lennon would later embrace wholeheartedly during his peace campaigns with Ono.

Arthur Ballard, a former tutor at the Art College commented that "without Stu Sutcliffe, John Lennon wouldn't have known Dada from a donkey" (Philip Norman, *John Lennon: The Life* p.136)

Late in 1959, Lennon's group sought to broaden their prospects for bookings with the addition of a drummer and/or bass player. Lennon allegedly tendered either role to Sutcliffe and fellow flat-mate and art student Rod Murray, who set about building a bass made from college materials. He was beaten to the role however by Sutcliffe who purchased a bass guitar sometime in early 1960 with £65 he made from the recent sale of a painting which had hung at exhibition in the prestigious Walker Art Gallery.

The general myth has always held that Sutcliffe was led astray by Lennon and the others, and duped into spending his money on the band. Quite the contrary however, it seems that Sutcliffe was a willing and enthusiastic addition to the group. Bill Harry claimed that the image of being in a rock 'n' roll band appealed to Sutcliffe more than the music itself, (Norman, Philip, Lennon, *The Life* p.168) and it became an extension of his own moody image. Lennon certainly approved, dismissing Sutcliffe's early struggles with his new oversized instrument by setting his priorities straight and declaring; "never mind, he looks good" (Norman, Philip, *John Lennon: The Life* p.237). George Harrison recalled that it was better to have a bass player who couldn't play, than not have one at all (*Anthology*).

Not everyone approved though. Paul McCartney smarted at his demotion in the ranks as a result of Lennon and Sutcliffe's friendship and he admitted years later that 'the others' were jeal-ous of the relationship, feeling they were forced to take a back seat (*Anthology*). In fairness, his dislike of the situation was also due to his frustrations with Sutcliffe's musical ability. Even at this early stage, the idealistic differences between Lennon, whose ethos was 'let's play', and McCartney who leaned towards 'let's play it right', were plain to see. Yet, it was the subtle marriage of these contrasting ideologies which would make their partnership so devastating throughout the decade.

So enthusiastic was Sutcliffe for his new life as a rock 'n' roller, that he began writing to booking agents on behalf of the band, and signed himself as—*manager*. Does that sound like the actions of a talented artist with a bright future, who was cajoled into parting with his money and joining a musical group with little prospects? Sutcliffe's next contribution to the group was to prove to be his most enduring. Still uncertain of their artistic moniker (The Quarrymen had Become Johnny and The Moondog's), Sutcliffe suggested The Beetles in homage to Buddy Holly's Crickets. This name evolved several times through Beetles, the Beatals, the Silver Beetles, The Beetles and finally, the Beatles.

In May 1960, the group famously auditioned to become a backing band for Billy Fury, but instead ended being assigned a drummer and embarking upon a budget tour of Scotland with Liverpool singer, Johnny Gentle. The tour was an eye-opener and a disaster for many reasons. For Sutcliffe however it revealed that the life of a musician was not necessarily glamorous, and that his friendship with Lennon was far from perfect.

Unable to compete with Sutcliffe's artistic abilities at college, Lennon seemed to enjoy becoming his friend's artistic superior once he strapped on a bass and stepped on-stage.

Lennon admitted that he was particularly cruel to Sutcliffe during the tour, refusing to allow him to eat or even sit with the others. He belittled his friend's height and zoned in on his struggles with the Höfner bass he wore.

By the time the group acquired permanent drummer Pete Best in August 1960, Sutcliffe found himself bound for Hamburg to play rock 'n' roll in the sleaziest of Europe's red light districts. He had horrified his family and tutors by abandoning his teacher training diploma and turned his back on his art completely. However he was held in such high regard by the Liverpool College of Art that they agreed to keep his place open for his return, if and when he saw fit.

For the others, no such friendly offers lay open . . . Hamburg was make or break.

Soon after his arrival on the Grosse Freiheit, Sutcliffe had met, fallen in love with and become engaged to a beautiful German existentialist by the name of Astrid Kircherr. Unlike the typical female fan, Kircherr was not only beautiful and stylish, but confident, cultured and a talented photographer.

The group were far from irritated by Sutcliffe's new found love, in fact they encouraged it. Kircherr's family acted somewhat like the Ashers later did for Paul McCartney. Mrs. Kircherr, appalled by the group's living conditions in St Pauli, allowed Stuart to lodge in the loft while often tending to the rest of the group; washing their clothes and providing hot meals. Astrid's affections and admiration for Sutcliffe's talent woke him from his rock 'n' roll coma and ignited his interest in art again. She and her friends also appealed to the existentialist in him, and it wasn't long before he was dressing just like his new German friends. In another vital building block to the group's image and direction, Sutcliffe became influenced by Hamburg's existentialists' clothing and hairstyles, and through him, so too did the Beatles.

Kircherr also took some iconic shots of the group, and her style was copied verbatim for the cover of their second LP; *With the Beatles*, which was considered an artistic watershed in terms of album covers.

Following the deportation of Harrison, McCartney and Best in late 1960, Lennon also headed for home leaving Sutcliffe behind with his fiancée. He had by now lost interest in his rock 'n' roll career and intended on taking up his studies again. Back in Liverpool the Beatles career began to take off following their first apprenticeship in Hamburg, and for a time they adapted a new bass player; Chas Newby, who later left of his own accord. In December of 1960, Harrison also apparently asked John Gustafson, bassist with the Big Three to join the Beatles . . . Gustafson declined, understandably a decision he lived to regret.

When Sutcliffe returned to Liverpool in February 1961 he headed straight for the Art College, committed to picking up where he left off. To his dismay he found the door firmly shut to him, regardless of his golden promise. The reason for his banishing was later discerned to be his suspected role in the misappropriation of a student's union amplifier; a Selmer Truvoice amp which was almost certainly 'borrowed' by The Silver Beetles. Disgusted and despondent, Sutcliffe returned to Hamburg in March 1961 to be with his fiancée and to test the possibilities of studying there. On application to the HFBK, or Hamburg College of Art, Sutcliffe made such an impression on Scottish-Italian artist and tutor Eduardo Paolozzi that he was immediately enrolled and given a generous grant. Sutcliffe soon picked up where he had left off in Liverpool by painting in the loft of the Kircherr house in Hamburg and, here his and the Beatles' paths began to diverge. He still occasionally played and sang with the group during their second Hamburg residency, but McCartney had by now largely taken over on bass.

By October 1961 Sutcliffe was suffering from blinding headaches and dark mood swings, often coupled with aggressive bouts of unprovoked jealousy towards his fiancée. He was eventually persuaded to see a doctor who diagnosed nothing but a troublesome appendix and advised Sutcliffe to slow down, rest and quit cigarettes and alcohol.

Early in 1962 his health declined further and he began suffering seizures. He was eventually diagnosed as suffering from increased cranial pressure and this was temporarily relieved by a treatment of cranial hydrotherapy. Sutcliffe and Kircherr visited Liverpool in February 1962, where friends noted his alarming weight loss and more than usual pale complexion.

During this visit he met Brian Epstein, the new Beatles manager, and discussed a future role as an artistic director and designer for the band. Predictably, Epstein was drawn to Sutcliffe's looks and later wrote to him in Hamburg that he "didn't know anyone as lovely as you existed in Liverpool" (Norman, *John Lennon: The Life* p.262).

Upon his return to Hamburg, Sutcliffe's seizures and mood swings escalated. He wrote home that "[his] head was compressed, and filled with such unbelievable pain" (Norman, *Lennon—The Life* p.262).

On April 10th 1962 he suffered an hour long seizure at his home and fell into a coma. Despite being rushed to hospital by ambulance Sutcliffe died during the journey, rested in his fiancée's arms. The next day, unaware of his death, the Beatles minus George Harrison flew out to Hamburg from Manchester to begin yet another engagement. They were greeted by a distraught Kircherr in the arrivals hall, and her news sent Lennon into aggressive hysterics. Lennon was later criticised by the Sutcliffe family however for his lack of emotion over his friend's death.

The show of emotion in Hamburg airport had evaporated—or been carefully withdrawn—by the time his friend's mother arrived (on the same flight as Harrison and Epstein) the following day. Lennon in his defence was 21 years old, hardly a matured man, and those young years had already seen their fair share of trauma. Already aware that his father and mother had abandoned him, death had been a frequent caller to his door what with losing his surrogate father (Uncle George) at 15, his mother at 17, and now his best friend at 21. It's little wonder that he developed an aggressive defence mechanism for bottling and hiding his emotions. There are enough clues throughout his life, however, to suggest that he was always haunted by the death of his best friend and perhaps his frequent cruel treatment of him in public. Kircherr felt his behaviour towards Sutcliffe was another of his defence mechanisms; "I'm thinking when he treated him badly, it was because he was afraid anyone might see how much he loved him" (Norman, *John Lennon: The Life*, p.214).

Sutcliffe may have been the subject of the confessional, self-healing and melancholy Beatles song "There's A Place," composed the same year as Sutcliffe's death. He was also certainly one of the central subjects in Lennon's 1965 autobiographical 'In My Life,' and his friend also ensured that Sutcliffe finally made it onto a Beatles album; standing among the greats of the 20th century on the cover of the group's magnum opus—*Sgt. Pepper's Lonely Hearts Club Band*.

Yoko Ono has also maintained that Lennon spoke of Sutcliffe every day throughout his life, so much so that she felt she had known him herself.

Controversy has surrounded Sutcliffe in death just as it has his deceased best friend. His death was deemed the result of a cerebral hemorrhage, but post mortem results pointed to a previous skull trauma, possibly the result of a blow . . . or a kick. Beatles myths often have a tendency to grow into monsters and Sutcliffe's death is no exception. Not surprisingly, views on how Sutcliffe may have been injured differ enormously.

The famous story is that Sutcliffe was ambushed and violently kicked in the head by a group of youths following a gig at Lathom Hall. This is the story put forth by Philip Norman, author of *Shout!* and *Lennon: The Life*. Norman states the incident occurred in early 1961, probably Feb 25th. He also states that Sutcliffe's mother found him that night, bleeding heavily from a head wound.

However, Bill Harry, Pete Best and Neil Aspinall maintained that the incident had occurred on May 14th 1960, and that it involved a few punches and nothing at all as sinister as a kick to the head. Best recalled; "When people talk of Stu being beaten up, I think it stems from this incident. But I don't remember Stu getting to the stage where he had his head kicked in, as some legends say, alleging that this caused his fatal brain haemorrhage" (*Mersey Beat* Archives).

The trouble is, neither Pete Best nor Neil Aspinall worked with the group in May 1960. They were both with the Beatles by February 1961 however, the time the incident occurred according to Philip Norman, although their recollections seem to refute the viciousness of Norman's description of events. Time has muddied the actual details it seems, but what probably occurred is that a minor fracas took place in February 1961, which involved no serious head injuries. Incidentally Sutcliffe only returned from Hamburg in late February 1961. So if he was with the group at this performance, it must have been one of his first engagements upon his return.

The Sutcliffe family have thrown further fuel on the fire in the debate. In her book *The Beatles' Shadow: Stuart Sutcliffe & His Lonely Hearts Club*, Sutcliffe's sister Pauline claims that on his final return to Liverpool her brother told his mother how John Lennon had attacked him in a drunken rage, knocking him to the ground and kicking him repeatedly in the head. The incident was supposedly fuelled by his jealousy of Stu, and his ever increasing frustrations with his musical abilities. Paul McCartney was cited as the sole witness, and it was allegedly he who carried a bleeding Sutcliffe back to his digs. The incident was kept in the Sutcliffe family until 1984, thus denying Lennon a chance to comment on the allegation of any involvement in his friend's death.

Lennon was known to have a violent streak, sure, and he was a famously mean drinker. However the alleged attack is largely out of character with his documented relationship with Sutcliffe, and indeed the rest of his band mates. There are well known stories of John Lennon going on-stage wearing a toilet seat, urinating from balconies, mugging sailors, and walking the streets in his underwear. So, surely a story of him administering a vicious beating to his best friend in public would be supported by someone who was there.

Horst Fascher, the group's unofficial bodyguard in Hamburg and a man for whom violence was a working tool, claims he never heard of such an incident. Sutcliffe himself, a man who wrote letters home frequently, never wrote of the incident, and neither Harrison nor Best has ever mentioned it. Astrid Kircherr, his fiancée, claims that Lennon never raised his hands to Sutcliffe, dismissing the allegation as "rubbish" (*The Lost Beatle*, BBC 4 Documentary).

McCartney, who supposedly witnessed the incident, has no recollection of it, although he admitted that John and Stuart *could* have had a drunken fight (*Anthology*). As always, analysis of recollections should be subjected to a degree of skepticism, owing to the sheer amount of time that has elapsed, not to mention the tricky issue of disentangling personal agenda.

McCartney has always come-off as a villain in Sutcliffe's story. The one well documented on-stage punch-up involving Sutcliffe was with McCartney, supposedly the result of an unkind comment aimed at Astrid Kircherr. He made no bones of his opinion on Sutcliffe's, and even Best's musical abilities, once shouting at them both during a performance; "You may look like James Dean and you may look like Jeff Chandler, but you're both crap" (Norman, *John Lennon: The Life*, p.237).

McCartney has confessed that he was jealous of Sutcliffe, the older boy, and no doubt Sutcliffe's image and artistic abilities intimidated the younger McCartney, as they had done Lennon.

In the Beatles *Anthology*, McCartney admits that his relationship with Sutcliffe grew particularly fraught, but Kircherr suggests it was more than that; ". . . when Paul and Stu had a row, you could tell that Paul hated him" (Norman, *Shout!*, p.90).

McCartney has always maintained that he never wanted the job as bass player, that he somehow got lumped with the job by the refusal of the others to take up the role. Harrison contradicted this, recalling that "He [McCartney] went for it [the bass role]" (*Anthology*).

Regardless, it seems that McCartney viewed Sutcliffe's departure as the best possible outcome for his and the band's collective gain . . . he was probably correct in his assessment. In any case, they did have options. Upon Sutcliffe's official departure from the group, Klaus Voorman, their Hamburg acquaintance who would design the cover of *Revolver* and play bass on numerous John Lennon solo albums, asked Lennon if he could take up the role as the Beatles bassist. Lennon turned him down telling him "sorry mate, Paul has already bought a bass . . . " (Mojo, *10 Years*, p.35).

It seems the allegations of Lennon's attack (as well as the predictable and highly irrelevant claims that Lennon and Sutcliffe had a homosexual relationship) are little but hearsay. But, they do sell books.

We will never know the true cause of Sutcliffe's haemorrhage, although no doubt the legend surrounding it will continue and grow. Kircherr was convinced that Stuart had an underlying condition that was lying in wait. That condition was possibly exacerbated by Sutcliffe's 24-hour lifestyle which has been documented by all those who knew him, tutors, musicians, lovers and friends. He simply worked too hard, too long, too intensely, smoked too much and ate and slept too little. In his last letters home he confessed how doctors had labelled him a nervous wreck.

But what of Sutcliffe's musical legacy? Was he the terrible bassist some would have us believe? Certainly, starting out in early 1960 he was very limited and struggled his way through the Scottish tour of May '60. However it's been well documented how the group went to Hamburg a 'banger' (jalopy) and came home a Rolls Royce . . . the relentless hours on stage turning them into a rock 'n' roll powerhouse. If Lennon, Best, Harrison & McCartney progressed as musicians, shouldn't it also follow that Sutcliffe did too? In 1960 Sutcliffe himself wrote home that the group had improved a thousand fold since their arrival in Hamburg ("Lost Beatle", BBC 4).

The surviving tapes that capture Sutcliffe on bass (*Anthology 1*) are too poor in quality to allow any real appreciation of his ability. So, we need to examine the recollections of those who were there.

McCartney's opinion has been well documented, but there were others and, contrary to the myth, many remember him as being highly competent on the instrument.

Klaus Voorman remembers Sutcliffe as being "a heavy rock 'n' roller. Rock 'n' roll is an art form, and Stuart had the feel and taste. They weren't playing anything very complicated, and taken as a whole—feeling it and playing those few notes—Stuart was a really, really, good bass player." (Mojo, *10 Years*, p.35).

Pete Best recalled how Sutcliffe was a decent musician with a good reputation among his Hamburg contemporaries, and Bill Harry (*Mersey Beat* founder) recalls that he was quite good. Furthermore, Sutcliffe sometimes played bass in a combo with Howie Casey (of the Seniors) in the Kaiserkeller, and they seemed to have no issue with his competency. (*Uncut* March 2012).

Sutcliffe, like Best, may have failed to make the grade when it came to the Beatles EMI career, in fact Best fell at the first hurdle. However in the case of both, it's been convenient to excuse their treatment by the group by highlighting their musical ineptitudes . . . but personal dislikes can't be ruled out of the equation either. The group closed rank on Best once George Martin flagged him, Sutcliffe was a different story however; he drifted out rather than having to be pushed. He had bigger fish to fry.

Some have argued that he wasn't talented enough to be in the Beatles, but his artistic pedigree meant that he was far too talented to be in the Beatles; in the world of painting rather than music. Sutcliffe knew when it was time to retire the bass and return to his canvass. Judging by the professional critique of his surviving work, Sutcliffe may well have enjoyed a successful career as an artist. In fact, had he never met John Lennon, nor joined the Beatles, Sutcliffe would possibly have become a successful artist regardless. The Beatles, though, benefited from his membership at a critical time in their transition from the rhythmless Quarrymen into the five piece who left for Hamburg and first played together as a band named 'the Beatles'. Sutcliffe and Best galvanised Lennon/McCartney/Harrison into a cohesive unit and allowed them to progress and mature as musicians and writers.

John Lennon always claimed that the best work of the Beatles was never captured, referring to their wild, pre-EMI days. If that's true, then he's referring to a period when it was more important to *play*, than what you played and who heard you. The rock 'n' roll played during this period was uncomplicated, and if Lennon's opinion counted for anything, and it should—it was his band after all—then the proto-punk stage material of 1960-1962 suited the talents of Pete Best and Stuart Sutcliffe more than adequately.

Sutcliffe's association with the Beatles would probably have catapulted him to the top of the artistic movements of the '60s as he lived a celebrity life with his beautiful German wife. Under his direction many of the group's album covers may have looked very different. Who knows, he may even have performed on a few of them.

∽

"A Portrait Of The Bassist: An Examination of Stuart Sutcliffe's Legacy With The Beatles 50 Years After His Death," Joe Rodgers. Copyright Dinosaur Album Guides.

[FOUR]

Janice the Stripper

By Paul McCartney

In their early years, getting practice and exposure was paramount for the fledgling Beatles. They often took whatever gig they could get—even if wasn't at the most refined venue. In this letter Paul sent to Mersey Beat, he talks about the time the boys played backup for Janice the Stripper, a well-endowed dancer who wouldn't work unless it was to the music of a live band. —L.M.

~

John, George, Stu and I used to play at a Strip Club in Upper Parliament Street, backing Janice the Stripper. At the time we wore little lilac jackets . . . or purple jackets, or something. Well, we played behind Janice and naturally we looked at her . . . the audience looked at her, everybody looked at her, just sort of normal. At the end of the act, she would turn round and . . . well, we were all young lads, we'd never seen anything like it before, and all blushed . . . four blushing red-faced lads.

Janice brought sheets of music for us to play all her arrangements. She gave us a bit of Beethoven and the Spanish Fire Dance. So in the end we said 'We can't read music, sorry, but instead of the Spanish Fire Dance we can play The Harry Lime Cha-Cha, which we've arranged ourselves, and instead of Beethoven you can have "Moonglow" or "September Song" —take your pick... and instead of the "Sabre Dance" we'll give you "Ramrod." So that's what she got. She seemed quite satisfied anyway.

The strip club wasn't an important chapter in our lives, but it was an interesting one.

∽

"A Little Bare," Paul McCartney. Originally published in Mersey Beat. Copyright Bill Harry.

[FIVE]

The Ed Sullivan Show

By David Bauder, Beth Harris and Frazier Moore

Hot off the heels of a successful string of hits in Britain that included Please Please Me, From Me to You, and She Loves You, the Beatles captivated the hearts of millions of people across the US with their American debut on The Ed Sullivan Show in 1964. The sound, look, and vibe of the Fab Four was unlike anything American audiences had ever seen—sparking a tidal wave of energy that began Beatlemania in the States. —L.M.

∿

It was 50 years ago today (almost) that this mop-topped band began to play (in America).

The Beatles made their first appearance on *The Ed Sullivan Show*, America's must-see weekly variety show, on Sunday, Feb. 9, 1964. And officially kicked off Beatlemania on this side of the pond. More than 70 million viewers were tuned to the program, airing live from the Manhattan studio now housing the *Late Show With*

David Letterman. Here are recollections from some notable viewers and participants—including one Beatle.

Charlie Brill and Mitzi McCall were an up-and-coming husband-and-wife comedy team that specialized in carefully crafted character sketches. They were thrilled when they landed their first appearance on *Sullivan.*

Unfortunately, they were booked on that first Beatles show—slotted just before the Beatles hit the stage for their second set. Needless to say, the studio audience—packed with teenage girls—wasn't interested in watching grown-ups doing comedy.

Charlie Brill: "Mr. Sullivan called us into his dressing room after dress rehearsal. He said, 'You're doing a very sophisticated piece of business and my audience is 14-year-old girls. They won't understand it. So why don't you show me everything you have, and we'll rebuild your whole act.'"

MM: "The biggest laugh we got was when I ad-libbed, 'I was backstage and I stepped on a beetle.'"

CB: "That got a roar."

MM: "And I thought, 'Oh, boy, are we in trouble!'"

CB: "After we finished, we stood in the wings and watched, but I couldn't hear anything. The screaming from the audience was so intense that I didn't even know what the Beatles were doing."

MM: "Now I feel like it was an honor to be on that show with them, but our performance wasn't what we wanted it to be. We never look at the recording of it."

At age 29, Vince Calandra was a rising young program coordinator on *The Ed Sullivan Show* whose many duties included, on one notable weekend, looking after four musical guests.

Fortunately, he was versatile.

"George was sick. He had a 102-degree temperature," says Calandra. "So he didn't come to the rehearsal that Saturday, and I stood in for him wearing a Beatles wig. When McCartney saw me with a guitar in my hand and a wig, he had a kind of look like, 'I'm glad you have a day job, 'cause you just don't look the part.'"

Standing just offstage for their performance that Sunday night, Calandra describes the sensation as "unnn-believable! Pannnn-demonium! You couldn't hear anything for the screaming."

The show culminated a long day at the theater, where the Beatles had arrived that morning.

"During the day, John seemed nervous, and basically sat around and doodled," Calandra says, "and kept asking for change for the Coke machine. Ringo was reading 'Green Hornet' and watching TV.

"They were all very professional, very respectful," sums up Calandra, who went on to have a long career as a producer. "They weren't like other groups that came in, whose attitude was, 'OK, let's do the *Sullivan Show* and sell a bunch of records and then on Monday morning we're all gonna go to the dealership and buy our new cars.' The Beatles really wanted this thing to work!"

Leslie Moonves was a teenager growing up on Long Island, N.Y., with no idea that he would one day run the network he was tuned to for *Ed Sullivan*.

In fact, just days before the historic broadcast, the CBS chairman and CEO had no idea whom the Beatles were.

"I remember the first time I heard the word 'Beatles,'" he recalls. "It was that Friday. I was in seventh grade and my best friend, who was really into music, said, 'You gotta watch them, they're on *The Ed Sullivan Show* on Sunday night.'

"I said, 'Really? There's a group called the Beatles?' It sounded gross.

"But I watched, and I saw this unbelievable crowd reaction to these guys. And at school the next day, the Beatles were all anybody was talking about. And I felt very cool, because I had seen it. But three days earlier, I hadn't heard of them."

These days, the Ed Sullivan theater is familiar territory for Moonves.

"I've done a number of presentations for advertisers from that stage," he says, adding that his mind immediately goes to the Fab Four. "(I think), 'The Beatles were here! The Beatles were here!' On these very planks beneath my feet."

Even Ringo Starr didn't know the magnitude of what was about to happen when he played with his bandmates that night. "Incredible!" he recalls. "It was *Ed Sullivan*, it was a big show. We didn't know while we were playing that 70 million people were watching, but it was being in America that was so exciting. "All the music we loved was in America, it came from America to England."

While holed up at their Manhattan hotel, they were interviewed by the city's leading deejays, which, all by itself, was an amazing experience.

"With Murray the K and Cousin Brucie, we were on the radio—we were in the hotel rooms on the phone to Murray the K. You didn't have anything like that in England. The whole experience was just incredible."

CBS anchor Walter Cronkite scored tickets to the *Sullivan Show* for his teenage daughters Nancy and Kathy.

"The Beatles were already huge, and huge to me—monumental!" Kathy Cronkite says. "The idea of seeing them in person was like going to another planet. And when we got there we were screaming our heads off, so we couldn't hear the music.

"Then, afterward, we got to meet them," she adds. "They were very nice. They put their arms around us for a picture, which was really fabulous. Ringo and I happened to be standing next to each other, and he was MY Beatle. So that was especially exciting."

For Cronkite, a former actress who appeared in the classic film *Network* but is now a mental-health advocate, many of the details have vanished with the passage of time.

"In the scope of the rest of my life, it has faded in significance somewhat," she says, but takes pains to emphasize, "I don't mean it wasn't important. At the time it was absolutely huge. And back then, when I was 13, I'm sure I thought it was the main thing that would EVER matter."

Pat DiNizio, lead singer of the New Jersey-based rock band the Smithereens, not only remembers seeing the Beatles on *Sullivan*, but also vividly recalls the first moment he heard their music.

He was 8 years old, brushing his teeth with his red transistor radio on when the disc jockey announced he was playing "I Want to Hold Your Hand." Stunned by the sound, he dropped the toothbrush. He watched the show from the living room of his home in Scotch Plains, N.J., with his parents.

"I wanted to be them. I wanted to do what they did. I wanted to have my haircut like that and I wanted to be in a rock 'n' roll band," he says. "That was a major, major important event for the youth of America. My parents couldn't have been over 30 years old and they didn't dig the Beatles too much. They didn't dig the long hair."

In 2006, the Smithereens released "Meet the Smithereens," a note-for-note remake of "Meet the Beatles," which was a strong seller online because the Beatles' music wasn't available through iTunes at the time. The Smithereens just released a new disc that is a run-through of the songs the Beatles played during their first concert on American soil, in Washington, D.C., on Feb. 11, 1964.

Singer-songwriter Rosanne Cash, Johnny's daughter, was 8 years old in 1964. She lived in southern California with her mother, Vivian, who was separated from Johnny by then.

"I loved the Beatles so much it was physically painful," she says. "I knew they were going to be on *Ed Sullivan* and I counted the minutes. When it was time, I sat in front of the television at least a half-hour before the show started because I was anxious that I might miss even a single second.

"When they were about to come on, my mother kept my sisters in the kitchen to keep them quiet, and I overheard her say, 'SHHH. Rosanne is watching the Beatles.' It was one of the greatest things my mom ever did for me." Cash has recorded versions of the Beatles' songs "I'm Only Sleeping" and "I Don't Want to Spoil the Party."

≈

[SIX]

Beatlemania Mystifies Grownups

By Arthur Everett, Cynthia Lowry and Associated Press Staff

Beatlemania was an unparalleled phenomenon in its time, and even to the present day has not had a true equivalent in terms of scope and cultural impact. This Associated Press reporting describes both the enormity of the crowds of fans—and the utter bewilderment of the older generation. —L.M.

In February 1964, the Beatles took America by storm, and rock 'n' roll was never the same.

AP reporters covering the band's Feb. 7 arrival at New York's Kennedy Airport and their appearance on *The Ed Sullivan Show* two days later never failed to mention John, Paul, George and Ringo's long hair, or the screaming teenage girls who followed them wherever they went.

In covering the airport arrival, AP reporter Arthur Everett goes to great lengths to use contemporary slang like "way out" and "fab."

And he quotes female fans as shouting "We want beatniks!" Might it have been "We want Beatles!"? The story on the Sullivan show appearance focuses on the scene, making scant mention of the band's music. In a separate review, AP television-radio writer Cynthia Lowry allows that the boys "sing close harmony." But she is put off by their hairdos, and declares that the appeal of the Liverpudlians remains a mystery to an "elderly viewer." (Lowry was in her early 50s at the time.)

Fifty years after their original publication, the AP is making these reports available to subscribers:

∾

BEATLES LAND IN NEW YORK
NEW YORK, Feb. 7 (AP)—Britain's way out Beatles, equipped with rag mop hairdos and guitars, invaded the colonies today. Thousands of delirious teen-aged native girls paid them wild tribal homage when they landed at Kennedy airport.

"I love them, I love them," shrieked one junior miss, teetering on the verge of emotional collapse. A singing quartet of British youth, the Beatles are all the rage—or rather "fab" for fabulous—on the tight little isle, and their fame has spread to America via best-selling recordings. Now they are here in person for a series of sold-out public appearances.

The Beatles collectively are sort of a sheep dog version of Elvis Presley—the adulation they arouse in reminiscent of the grip the American star once held on the juvenile population.

However, when a newsman described them to their faces—or the visible portions thereof—as "four Elvis Presleys," they replied in unison: "Not True."

As the Beatles left their transatlantic airliner shortly after noon, 5,000 school-skipping American fans stormed police barricades, pelted the quartet with jelly beans and candy kisses, and screamed: "We want beatniks! We want beatniks!"

Behind them, with their departure from London, the Beatles left a pack of British teen-age girls, awash in tears, keening forlornly and twisting sodden hankies in anguished farewell.

But accustomed as they are to the weird worship rites attending their every appearance, the Beatles were shocked into momentary immobility as they left their plane to face the American horde. They recovered enough to wave, mug and dance a small jig for their panting audience.

"It's marvelous," Beatle Paul McCartney, 21, later told a news conference. "It's fantastic! We've never seen or had anything like this before. It's the best ever."

There was some small measure of mild dissent amid the joyous welcoming uproar that kept 100 policemen on edge at the airport. One sign on display read: "Beatles go home!" and another proclaimed: "We love Beethoven."

At the news conference the Beatles were informed that a "stamp out the Beatles" movement is under way in Detroit.

"We're going to start a campaign to stamp out Detroit," was their rejoinder.

As for Beethoven, Beatle Ringo Starr, 23, conceded that "he's beat—especially his poems."

～

ED SULLIVAN APPEARNCE

NEW YORK, Feb. 9 (AP)—The Beatles—four British Lads who sing when they are not busy running away from barbers—made their American Television debut tonight—and some things may never be the same.

The seats in the Columbia Broadcasting System studio where they appeared live on the *Ed Sullivan* variety show were given more of a workout by jumping and squirming teenaged girls than were the singers in their fast-moving routine.

The four mop-topped entertainers, who came here Friday from London, provided their own musical background with string and percussion instruments.

Throughout their two appearances during the show, the 721 members of the audience—mostly young girls—kept up a steady stream of squeals, sighs and yells.

The four British imports, appearing for a total of about 20 minutes on the hour-long show, may well have ended up with second billing. Camera crews were lavish in their shots of the audience, showing young girls leaping from their seats, throwing their arms into the air and staring bug-eyed. Some appeared as if on the verge of coma, staring open-mouthed.

At one point before the program, there was some doubt that the four singers would be able to make their way into the studio through the masses of teenage fans trying for a glimpse of their idols.

But hundreds of Manhattan Police, including mounted officers, shoved back the eager fans and cleared a path for the four entertainers.

Fans also gathered outside the Plaza Hotel in sunny, freezing weather as the performers went back and forth earlier in the day to rehearse at the studio.

Following the afternoon rehearsal, the Beatles recorded three numbers for an *Ed Sullivan* show to be aired Feb. 23. They will be on the show next Sunday, live from Miami Beach, Fla. The Beatles will also give concerts in Washington, D.C., and in New York.

On Saturday, George Harrison, lead guitarist of the Beatles, was confined to the hotel with a sore throat while drummer Ringo Starr and guitarists John Lennon and Paul McCartney rehearsed and toured New York by car.

The Beatles wear mushroomed shape hairdos down to their eyebrows and tight black suits. In America they currently have the top selling album and the number one and three top selling single records, "I Want to Hold Your Hand" and "She Loves You."

REVIEW: FOR TEENAGE GIRLS ONLY

NEW YORK, Feb. 10 (AP)—Anyone who is not a teen-age girl obviously is unqualified to comment on the sight of the Beatles in action.

Heaven knows we've heard them enough. It has been impossible to get a radio weather bulletin or time signal without running into "I Want to Hold Your Hand."

And now, having seen the four performers on *Ed Sullivan*'s CBS show last night, Beatlemania is even more of a mystery to an elderly viewer.

They sing close harmony, stomp their feet and play electric guitars, but so do a lot of crew-cut American boys in slacks and sweaters, and they cause no riots.

Beatle clothes look about two sizes too small, and I've seen Hungarian sheep dogs with more attractive hairdos.

But thousands of squealing young girls get their message. Camera shots of panting youngsters in Sullivan's audience were disquieting, in fact.

Maybe after two more exposures to the Beatles on television, all of us elderly people will become Beatlenuts, yeah, yeah, yeah, but I doubt it.

∽

[SEVEN]

Why Did Girls Go So Crazy for the Beatles?

By Jordan Gaines Lewis

The shrieking multitudes chasing John, Paul, George, and Ringo like prey is the stuff of legend. We know the lads were fantastic, but what exactly was it about them that turned their female (and some male) fans into mindless zombies? Jordan Gaines Lewis of Pennsylvania State University attempts to find the answer. —L.M.

This Sunday marks the 50th anniversary of John, Paul, George, and Ringo's debut appearance on *The Ed Sullivan Show* in the US. But what was it about? Was it the moptop haircuts, Cuban heels, and "*yeah yeah yeahs*" that turned us, our parents, or our grandparents into primeval beings whose sole purpose was to drown out the blare of a Vox AC30 amplifier?

The term "Beatlemania" has come to be associated with many things over the past half-century. Coined in October 1963 during the Beatles' tour of Scotland, the extent of Beatlemania in the US is obvious from record sales alone. Between the 1964 release of I Want to Hold Your Hand on the Billboard Hot 100 and the *Let it Be* EP in 1970, the Lads from Liverpool had a Number One single for, on average, one out of every six weeks and a top-selling album every third week.

But to most, Beatlemania conjures up a vivid image of frenzied fans, predominantly teenage girls, with facial expressions that look more like they'd witnessed a gruesome murder, and "I love George!" badges hanging on for dear life as their owners attempted to push past overwhelmed human police barricades. Lots of tears and lots of screaming.

But what can neuroscience tell us about what might have been happening in their brains?

Why do we like music? One could argue that fanatics were interested in more than just the Beatles' musical talent, but record sales prove that people did enjoy a Beatles tune. And what about music can make us tap our toes, lulls babies to sleep, well up with emotion, dance around or stir up furious mosh pits?

In short, we know music makes us feel good; even those tunes that incite a feeling of sadness may bring us pleasure because we can relate to them. Take one 2001 study by researchers Anne Blood and Robert Zatorre at McGill University. They recruited ten individuals who had at least some formal music training. Each participant selected a song that, they claimed, gave them (good) chills.

The researchers played a 90-second excerpt of their chosen song while the subject laid in a magnetic resonance imaging (MRI) machine, a device that measures brain activity by detecting changes in blood flow. Compared to control (neutral) sounds, music that elicits physical and emotional changes activated limbic, paralimbic, and midbrain regions. And these areas are implicated in pleasure and reward, not unlike the neural pathways that recognise yummy food, addictive drugs, and sex.

In an extension to this study published last April, Zatorre's group used fMRI to scan the brains of 19 volunteers while they listened to the first 30 seconds of 60 songs they'd never heard before. Participants then rated how much they were willing to spend if they were to buy each song, from $0 to $2.

As it turns out, connections between a limbic system structure called the amygdala with the hippocampus (involved in learning and memory) as well as the prefrontal cortex (important for decision-making) could predict how much participants were willing to spend on each song.

The strength of these connections may partially explain why diehard Metallica fans might completely shun hip-hop, while others may refuse to listen to anything but country. Music is a personal preference, and although we know that it brings us pleasure, that's about the extent of our understanding.

What's with all the crying and fainting? Typically, we equate crying with sadness and fainting with illness.

The truth is, our brains are actually pretty dumb, and any sudden, strong emotion—from happiness to relief to stress—can elicit these vulnerable physical reactions.

Our autonomic nervous system (the "involuntary" nervous system) is divided into two branches: sympathetic ("fight-or-flight") and parasympathetic ("rest-and-digest"). Acting via the hypothalamus, the sympathetic nervous system is designed to mobilise the body during times of stress. It's why our heart rate quickens, why we sweat, why we feel ready to run. The parasympathetic nervous system, on the other hand, essentially calms us back down.

The parasympathetic nervous system does something funny, too. Connected to our lacrimal glands (better known as tear ducts), activation of parasympathetic receptors by the neurotransmitter acetylcholine results in tear production. So for those fans relieved to finally see their Fab Four, tears were commonplace.

For others, though, the sudden activation of their parasympathetic nervous system is accompanied by something much more dramatic. A quick drop in blood pressure results from vessels widening and heart rate slowing, hence the fainting.

Fainting, crying . . . exactly the things you'd want your hero to see you do when you finally meet them, right?

Everybody's crazy 'bout a sharp-dressed man: Let's be honest, there's a reason Beatlemania is typified by hordes of young women: *The Beatles looked good.*

When Brian Epstein officially signed on as the Beatles' manager in early 1962, the first thing he did was smarten up their stage appearance; he fitted them into Edwardian collarless suits, matching boots, and choreographed a synchronised bow at the end of each song.

According to a 2011 survey, 91% of Americans believe that a well-dressed man appears smarter, sexier, and more successful than one who is not, regardless of their overall physical attractiveness or how much money they have.

And a 1990 study of 382 college students by the University of Toledo examined just how clothes can make the man. One "attractive" and one "unattractive" man (as previously determined by a panel of females) donned a variety of clothes—from designer watches and pressed shirts to baseball caps and Burger King polos. Consistently, women rated the well-dressed man as more attractive than the sloppier one, regardless of which model sported which ensemble.

The Beatles had some pretty great hair, too. Inspired by a man they saw during a gig in Hamburg, Germany, John and Paul reportedly hitchhiked to Paris and requested the distinctive haircut.

Across cultures, long, shiny female hair is rated attractive by both genders. Evolutionary psychologists reason that the ability to grow long hair can reveal several years of a person's health status, age, nutrition, and reproductive fitness, as vitamin deficiencies result in hair loss.

Plus, moptops eliminate any sign of androgenic alopecia, or male-pattern baldness, which studies have been associated with perceived ageing and less attractiveness. But don't worry, men—evolutionary biologists theorise that baldness is actually a sign of dominance, longevity, and social status due to its cause—a more potent form of testosterone called DHT.

Although the fans may have drowned out the music with their shrieks, at least they still had a sight to behold.

So 50 years ago this Sunday, 73m Americans crowded around

60% of the country's televisions to watch the Beatles' debut, and the birth of Beatlemania. But while there are some explanations for why frenzied fans might have reacted the way they did to the Fab Four, for some the teenage shrieks and hysteria remained utterly baffling.

∼

"Beatlemania Hit 50 Years Ago But Why did it Drive Girls so Mad?," Jordan Gaines Lewis. Originally published on The Conversation.

[EIGHT]

Chasing the Fab Four Around D.C.

By Ron Oberman

The seismic waves of the Beatles' popularity were immediately felt everywhere, including in the American capital. Here, one record industry insider talks about what it was like covering the Beatles' D.C. performance as a young journalist in '64. —L.M.

~

The Beatles came to town on Feb. 11, 1964, to play at the old Washington Coliseum, their first U.S. show ever . . .I was at that debut, as well as at the band's press conference earlier that day at the Coliseum.

That week Washington's Top 40 AM radio stations were still blaring such hits as Lesley Gore's You Don't Own Me" on WEAM, Diane Renay's "Navy Blue" on WEEL, Andy Williams' "A Fool Never Learns" on WPGC, the Rip Chords' "Hey Little Cobra" on WWDC, and Dionne Warwick's "Anyone Who Had a Heart" on WINX.

At the same time, "She Loves You" and "I Want to Hold Your

37

Hand" had already begun making inroads on radio stations through-out the metropolitan area.

As the new sensations from England hit the stage at the Coliseum on that cold Tuesday night in February, they should have felt right at home: The venue was no more than a large version of the famed Cavern Club in Liverpool, where they got their start.

The Coliseum was dark, dank, and equipped with a primitive sound system. The group's amplified vocals and instruments fought to be heard over the fans' frenzied screams. The frenzied screams won, hands down.

Still, here was a band unlike any I had ever seen. They were four distinct personalities. They looked like emissaries from the future: You could not take your eyes off their haircuts and clothing. Most important, they wrote their own songs, music unlike that of any rock 'n' roll act I had ever heard. It was pure musical magic.

At the time, I was a 20-year-old who wrote the weekly music column, "Top Tunes," in the "Teen" section of the *Washington Evening Star*. Each Friday, I would write about a hot act on the music scene.

When it was announced that the Beatles would be doing a press conference prior to their show at the Coliseum, I approached one of the city editors at the *Star* and asked if I could cover the event for the daily paper, as opposed to waiting until my music column came out. I was bigfooted: A more senior writer had already been assigned to chronicle the Beatles' whirlwind visit to Washington.

Naturally, I was disappointed, but I understood. I was still in school at the University of Maryland and only working part time at the *Star* as a dictationist (who, before computers, sat at a bank of typewriters and, using a headphone, transcribed stories phoned in by reporters). I was glad just to be going to the press conference and the concert.

Not wanting to wait until the last minute to pick up my press credentials, I rose early on the day of the concert and headed for the Coliseum at 3rd and M streets in Northwest. It had been snowing that day and, in my haste and excitement to get there, I skidded on some ice a block from the hall, and rear-ended another car.

So you see, the inability of D.C. drivers to operate motor vehicles in the snow is no laughing matter: It almost made me miss the Beatles' first U.S. concert.

Fortunately, in this case the damage was minor: I made it to the Coliseum a few minutes after exchanging information with the other driver. Oh, and nobody was injured. Now I live in Southern California, where I can't hurt anybody.

Arriving late for their pre-show press conference, the Beatles strode into a boxing ring in the center of the Coliseum, unleashing sheer media frenzy. Flashes were popping constantly, and the group was barraged with questions.

I had a several-minute conversation with John Lennon. I asked him how he and Paul McCartney write the group's songs. "Generally, we like off-tempo, happy songs," he said, little anticipating the sophistication and universal appeal of so many of their more mature later efforts. "We just sit down, bang them out and hum the tunes."

Throughout the approximately 20-minute press meeting, the band was polite and characteristically impish. I recall asking George Harrison, "Do you currently have a girlfriend." His reply? "Yes, love, you."

As showtime neared, the foursome's road manager halted the questioning so they could rest for a couple hours in their hotel rooms. Mr. Lennon was in the middle of answering a question of mine and, as the manager towed him by the arm up the stairs of the Coliseum, he continued to shout back the answer until I was out of hearing range. I never did hear the rest of his reply.

The Beatles took the stage at about 9:30 p.m. and played for about 45 minutes, a short, 12-song set by today's standards. I saw the performance, but I can't say I heard it.

It's a safe assumption that they played "I Want to Hold Your Hand," but the dozens of police, security and ushers working the event just wanted to plug their ears. Unprepared for the deafening roar of the crowd packed inside the Coliseum, many of them resorted to stuffing Kleenex or cotton—anything they could find—in their ears.

I later covered Beatles shows for the Star in Baltimore, Atlantic City, Los Angeles, and another in the District. The second Washington show, attended by about 30,000, was held on Aug. 15, 1966, at the old D.C. (later RFK) Stadium. It was immediately preceded by a press conference held inside the locker room of the Washington Senators baseball team.

The questions at this press conference were more knowing than those from the Coliseum more than a year previously (a long time in the increasingly short cycles of pop culture), and the band, although not as witty and playful this time around, was gracious and respectful of the press in attendance.

A sample question: Have the Beatles thought much about eventually breaking up? "We've realized the possibility of breaking up," Mr. McCartney admitted, quickly adding that it would come as part of the "natural progression" of any group.

Amid some of the tightest security ever seen at an event in Washington, the Beatles came on at 9:35 p.m. and performed 11 songs in 35 minutes. It's hard to believe that this was just a few years before 35-minute drum solos became commonplace at rock concerts.

It wouldn't be the last time I saw the Beatles. Prior to their concert at the Baltimore Civic Center concert on Sept. 13, 1964, I waited for an hour outside their rooms at the Holiday Inn with Carroll James, the late WWDC disc jockey who was the first to play the Beatles music in Washington. Eventually, all four came out and schmoozed with us and posed for pictures for several minutes.

But nothing could compare to that very first U.S. date on Feb. 11, 1964, when four young Englishmen took the stage at the Washington Coliseum—then took the nation and the world and never let go.

I still wish I knew what the rest of John Lennon's answer to my question was. Hope it wasn't anything important.

[NINE]

How the Beatles Redefined Pop Celebrity

By Martin King

The Hard Day's Night film was a smash hit upon release; teens dug the chance the see the Fab Four on the silver screen while adults enjoyed the witty critique of Beatlemania. In this piece, Martin King of Manchester Metropolitan University asserts that the Beatles were the first celebrities in the modern sense. There had been stars before, but the Beatles went beyond stardom to become lasting molders and shapers of public consciousness. —L.M.

∼

July 6 2014 marked the 50th anniversary of the Royal Charity Premiere of *A Hard Day's Night*, the Beatles' first feature film. With its mock-documentary format, it captures a day in the life of the Beatles at the height of Beatlemania (the film's working title), and the true beginning of modern celebrity—a kind of fame that went far beyond what had gone before, and certainly beyond the Beatles' music itself.

The Beatles are the ultimate symbol of the 1960s, and were already part of the cultural zeitgeist in 1964, magnifying and reflecting that which they embraced. To this day their music provides a soundtrack to a version of the 1960s, real or imagined, where we seem happy to return again and again.

Film theorists and cultural historians have long revered *A Hard Day's Night* as a key 1960s text; on its release, it was famously described in the *Village Voice* as "the *Citizen Kane* of jukebox musicals". But for the 12,000 fans who screamed outside the premiere and those who subsequently paid to see it at their local cinema, it simply offered the chance to see and hear their heroes up close.

So why were and are the Beatles so famous—and why, 50 years on, do we still care? The answer, I would argue, lies in the period in which Beatlemania took root.

Right place, right time: Beatlemania was a unique convergence of the media, fans, and a cultural phenomenon in the right place at the right time. 1964 saw the publication of Marshall McLuhan's *Understanding Media*, which (among other things) introduced us to the concept of the "global village". Changes such as the rising ownership of TVs in British homes and the resurgence of the British film industry both played a key part in the Beatles' international success—and allowed the Beatles, in turn, to become global standard-bearers for the UK.

They were, according to music journalist Ian MacDonald, the perfect "McLuhanites", made for the new visual media. They were a gang, full of youthful exuberance and wit, Northerners, and talented. They perfectly embodied the emerging theme of upward social mobility and the idea of a new classless society, and were the epitome of the new meritocracy.

They were men of ideas, breaking down the popular/intellectual divide through their engagement with other art forms; that only increased as the decade progressed; books, films, TV shows and the avant-garde and satire movements would all form part of their starnet as the decade progressed.

Yet, paradoxically, while the Beatles did dramatically subvert the traditional expectations of pop stars, another major part of their success was much more conventional: the foursome's close relationship and commitment to their fan club, which played a big part in fostering the adoration and fan–worship of the Beatlemania period.

Cut your hair! Another often overlooked factor was the version of masculinity the Beatles represented, which was explicitly resistant to the norm. A certain gender fluidity was part of their appeal to both sexes. To the fans, they offered four different aspects of masculinity: pick your favourite—the acerbic John, baby-faced, pouting Paul, quiet and spiritual George, or Ringo, the ordinary one.

Their most obvious challenge to the traditional masculine image was the mop-top hairstyle, a feminised style which owed much to the US 1960s girl groups, and a song-writing style which often spoke to the perspective of the female fan. "She Loves You", perhaps the core of the Beatlemania period, takes the form of a conversation between two men about relationships. The refrain "You should be glad" predated the concept of the new man by 20 years. All of this is at its feverish height in "A Hard Day's Night".

In the *Twilight Zone* episode "Walking Distance", Gig Young stars as businessman Martin Sloane who, worn down by modern living, finds himself back in the town of his childhood where nothing has changed. Maybe that's what keeps drawing us back to Beatlemania: a nostalgia for simpler times—real or imagined.

And yet, the cultural phenomenon of the Beatles has changed and adapted to fit right into the 21st century. In McLuhan's global village made real, iTunes, Youtube, Amazon and ebay all provide platforms for 21st-century Beatlemania to flourish, 50 years on. Still the perfect McLuhanites.

As the band's longtime press officer Derek Taylor put it when announcing their breakup in 1970: "The Beatles are not a pop group; they are an abstraction, a repository for many things."

"A Hard Day's Night at 50: How John, Paul, George, and Ringo Redefined Pop Celebrity," Martin King. Originally published on The Conversation.

[TEN]

The Mysterious Chord from "A Hard Day's Night"

By Jason Brown

There are few chords in rock as singular and recognizable as the one that opens "A Hard Day's Night." But what chord is it exactly? Many a Beatles tribute band has tried to get it down pat to no avail. Mathematician Jason Brown is on a quest to identify the mysterious chord—will he succeed where others have failed?
—*L.M.*

∾

"TWANG! It's been a . . . " There is perhaps no song as quintessentially Beatle-ish as "A Hard Day's Night" —it just bubbles with unbridled enthusiasm and joy. And in my mind, there's no other opening chord of a rock song that is as instantly recognisable as that one.

I grew up grudgingly playing the piano, practising only the half-hour before my lesson each week. But as soon as I heard my first Beatles' record, I dropped the piano to teach myself guitar eight

44

hours a day during my high school summers. Something about the early Beatles' music struck a chord, so to speak, deep down inside of me, and it hasn't left.

At about the same time, my love for mathematics blossomed, and I played in a band while attending my undergraduate studies. It was a tough choice, but I gave up music for the safer gig, as a mathematician. But unbeknown to me, the music that lay dormant inside me would serendipitously mix with the math inside me.

In 2004 I heard it was the 40th anniversary of the Beatles' first movie—*A Hard Day's Night*—and the soundtrack of the same name. All of the media attention brought to mind that famous opening chord that opened the movie and title song.

While teaching myself guitar years earlier, I had invested in a lot of Beatles songbooks, only to find that every book had a different transcription for how the author thought George Harrison had coaxed that initial sound out of his brand new twelve-string Rick-enbacker guitar. All were derived by some combination of listening and music theory, but to me none sounded quite right.

My mathematical outlook had me take a different approach in 2004—was there a scientific way to decide how the chord was played? Indeed, I had read a math book for leisure (yes we mathematicians do that sort of thing!) about ten years earlier that described the mathematics of sound and music.

In particular, there was a process, called a Fourier transform, that could allow one to decompose a sound wave into its constitute pure tones (which were modelled by sine and cosine curves). I had also remembered that there were algorithms to do just that, so I embarked on some CSI-like musical forensics. I took a small part of the opening chord and ran it through a Fourier transform, and held my breath waiting for the output.

It was a bit daunting—there were thousands of frequencies in the opening chord. But all was not lost, as I could tell the amplitudes of the frequencies, and the amplitude corresponds roughly with the loudness. So I began to make mathematical deductions from the data, and I quickly came upon some interesting conclusions.

First, all of the transcriptions I had seen for the guitar chord were incorrect—they had a low G note present, and the mathematics clearly indicated that the frequency simply wasn't present.

Musicians thought they had heard the note, and as the key of the song was G, they believed it to be there all the more strongly. But it wasn't.

Furthermore, I could see that the frequencies often were not particularly close to notes, so that it would have behoved the Beatles' producer, George Martin, to have knocked on the studio window before the final take of the song and said: "Better tune up again, boys." The Beatles' guitars were gloriously slightly out-of-tune, adding to the difficulty in reproducing the chord.

A much bigger problem loomed. There were three frequencies corresponding to a certain "F" note, with no corresponding note up the octave, and this meant that note couldn't have been played on George Harrison's twelve string, and further, there was no way for the Beatles' guitars to cover the frequencies. The answer involved throwing out the assumption that only the Beatles played on the opening chord.

A solution lay with insertion of a piano into the mix, as pianos have, toward the top end of the keyboard, three identically tuned strings under each note. Upon this realisation, the remainder of the chord began to unravel fairly quickly, and I could deduce what instruments (guitars, bass and piano) played what notes. A little bit of math went a long way!

The greatest difficulty I encountered after the research was finding a public forum to publish the work. It was going to appear in a peer-reviewed journal, but I thought the story was interesting enough for everyone to read. One magazine refused to read it based on the fact that the article had mathematics in it! But *Guitar Player* magazine loved the work, and was happy to publish the article, and the rest is, as they say, history.

Over the ensuing years, I have applied mathematics in a variety of ways to analyse pop music. In a second article in Guitar Player magazine I deduced mathematically that George Harrison must have recorded his famous, brilliant solo in "A Hard Day's Night" by slowing down the tape speed in half, and recording the solo at half-speed down the octave.

Some musicians I've spoken with have been upset at the research, as perhaps it showed George's technical skills were not what they should have been, but the truth I think says more—it showed George was a musician first, doing what it took to play what was in his head rather than in his fingers, and he had to have an incredible amount of confidence to choose to record a solo at half-speed, knowing that all of the world would be watching for when he played it up to speed, live (which, of course, he did!).

I've also written about why the music to "I Want To Hold Your Hand" was so imaginative and clever that it brought America to its knees, and why Paul McCartney so correctly named Little Richard's "Long Tall Sally" as perhaps one of the greatest rock songs ever (and more generally, a mathematical basis for why the blues chord progression is so damn good).

Finally, in recent work with Robert Dawson of St. Mary's University, we explained mathematically why George Martin's famous edit in Strawberry Fields Forever never quite satisfied Paul (and never could).

Moreover, the research continues to open doors for me, especially as an ambassador for mathematics. I've written a book for the general public called *Our Days Are Numbered: How Mathematics Orders Our Lives* and published my first CD, *Songs in the Key of Pi*, of my own songs.

In fact, the Wall Street Journal came a-knocking back in 2008, and shot a video of a song I wrote in the style of the early Beatles, using mathematical principles I gleaned from their music.

And I continue to travel worldwide, giving public lectures on mathematics and music, most often with a guitar slung over my shoulder and with a rockin' band behind me. The Beatles, it seems, gave me a great ticket to ride!

～

"A Hard Day's Night Decoded: The Beatles by the Numbers," Jason Brown. Originally published on The Conversation.

[ELEVEN]

Ringo Hates Donald Duck

By Ringo Starr

We often think of John, Paul, and George—the three Beatle songwriters—as the primary objects of fans' adulation. But Ringo, with his unique nose and peculiar sense of humor, had many-a-follower as well. Here, he describes his handling of the lavish gifts bequeathed him by his admirers. —L.M.

∽

I collect most of the souvenirs which are sent to me, and also some which are sent to the rest of the group. I like them all and I think the fans are good for sending them to us.

I've got most of them on a shelf in the house and have about sixty dolls. I've got dogs, fish, kewpie dolls, elephants, and on my birthday I received a model of Fred Flintstone which actually plays a bass drum—he is fabulous.

Many of the presents which are sent to us are handmade and I appreciate what the girls have made themselves.

I like everything that's sent along—except Donald Duck! and because I don't like Donald Duck—I've got fifteen Donald Duck's! We receive every kind of present and I have rings and bracelets from fans, but the amount of jelly babies sent to us is tremendous— we couldn't possibly eat them all.

∽

"Among my Souvenirs," Ringo Starr. This article was originally published in Mersey Beat. Copyright Bill Harry.

[TWELVE]

Ringo: The Beat of the Beatles

By James Rosen

Some say Ringo Starr was less integral to the Beatles than the other members of the band. But anyone who knows a thing or two about music will tell you that Ringo shook up rock drumming. —L.M.

∽

R ingo Starr replaced the famously ousted Pete Best as the Beatles' drummer in August 1962, on the eve of the band's dazzling emergence from Liverpool.

A myth has long persisted that because Ringo was the last to join the group, he was just lucky, incidental to the Beatles' sound and success.

Today, the man who put the beat in Beatles is fast approaching 65. He has, according to published reports, undergone three shoulder surgeries this year just to be able to continue playing the drums in that familiar, cross-handed, deceptively simple way of his.

Earlier this month, Capitol released the Beatles' first four

American albums on compact disc, in mono and stereo. September saw the publication of Ringo's own valentine to his old mates—"Postcards From the Boys" (Chronicle Books), a coffee-table book reproducing the fronts and backs of alternately sweet, silly and sad dispatches he received from his fellow Beatles spanning 1965 to the mid-'90s.

Ringo's book of postcards, paradoxically enough, reinforces the stubborn misconception that his three great claims to fame are named John, Paul and George.

The postcards from his friends might feed the myth—but those early albums he recorded with them don't.

There's one thing about the Beatles that still needs to be said. It can fit on a postcard: Ringo Starr was a musical genius. His drumming revolutionized pop music and was indispensable to the Beatles' artistic alchemy and commercial dominance.

It is a tribute to this legendary performer's self-effacing nature—his unassuming personality and uncanny knack for knowing how much, or how little, was needed to build and release tension in a song—that the world has showered every last superlative on the Beatles' output without ever fully recognizing the contribution of the fourth man, the noncomposer, the novelty vocalist—the comic relief.

The myth holds that the Fab Four could have made it with any passable yahoo planted behind them, simply keeping the beat to those indestructible Lennon-McCartney gems.

Didn't they replace Ringo on "Love Me Do"? Didn't some other guy (Name: Jimmy Nicol) put on the suit and play in Ringo's place for six tour dates in spring 1964? And didn't the girls scream just as loud? And didn't Paul McCartney play drums on "Ballad of John and Yoko"?

All true—and all irrelevant.

Ringo Starr revolutionized pop drumming not once, but twice.

Turn on oldies radio sometime, and give a close listen to the drumming on any top-40 hit from the PBE (pre-Beatles era). There is no comparison. It's a quantum leap from even the best of the lot to the muscularity, crisp, cracking sharpness, boxy backbeat bigness, the exciting, lunging aliveness that Ringo brought to—you name it—any up-tempo tune off those first four American albums.

There are only a handful of PBE hit songs that even approach—forget equal—the innovations Ringo wrought from 1963 to 1965. The drumming on the great '50s hits—seminal records by Chuck Berry, Little Richard, Elvis Presley and the rest—was rooted in the jazz-swing tradition, from which so many of the era's session drummers hailed.

In the early '60s, there were a few hints of what was to come: the Angels' "My Boyfriend's Back," with its interplay of snare drum and handclaps; Nino Tempo and April Stevens' "Deep Purple," with its steady, easy-rocking rhythm; and Frankie Valli and the Four Seasons' "Walk Like A Man," with its complex, constantly changing rhythms.

But these fade in comparison to the furious machine-gun precision on display in "Please Please Me," the rolling thunder and raining-cymbal attack on "She Loves You," the controlled chaos of "It Won't Be Long," the Latin-hard-rock fusion driving "I Feel Fine."

Simply put: No rock drummer had ever played quite the way Ringo did, with the combined strength of his snapping snare and bass-drum backbeat. He also offered unusual, convention-shattering fare such as the beats on "Ticket To Ride" and "In My Life."

By the time the wave caught up with Ringo—in the form of more technically proficient speed demons such as The Who's Keith Moon and percussive maestros including Led Zeppelin's John Bonham—the happy-go-lucky Beatle was already onto a whole new thing, also without equal in the charting pop music of the day. This was his elegant and highly intuitive exploitation of the tom-toms, not only for "fills"—the little spaces between chord changes where drummers typically show off—but as the continuous stuff of the song itself.

It started on "She Said, She Said," with its slurred, manic fills; grew on "Hello, Goodbye," where the fills began expanding into whole verses (check out what Ringo's playing while Paul sings "Why why why why why why do you SAY goodbye"); and reached its apex on songs such as "Come Together" and "Sun King," where Ringo virtually surfed during verses.

Modern Drummer magazine has recorded that Ringo is responsible for more people taking up the drums than any other musician in history, a fact that speaks as much to Ringo's art—his unique, damnably deceitful, head-swaying illusion of making it look easy—as to his proximity to John and Paul.

How many other artists—public figures of any stripe—can take a glance behind them and see so much created in their image?

∽

[THIRTEEN]

How *Help!* Helped Redefine Masculinity

By Martin King

Help!, the follow-up to A Hard Day's Night, takes a different approach than its predecessor—wackier, funnier and more absurd. The fatigue of non-stop touring and album-making was catching up to the Beatles at this point—their frustration is reflected in the downbeat tone of 64's Beatles for Sale—so they were probably relieved at the prospect of indulging in nonsensical fun for a time. Plus, they were high for a lot of the shooting. But the film's cultural significance goes beyond the zaniness. —L.M.

It's 50 years since the release of the Beatles's second feature film, *Help!*. Whatever you may think of the film itself (which got very mixed reviews) this rollicking film of "good, clean insanity" provides a wonderfully unique window on to the social changes that men saw in the 1960s.

As Alex Bilmes recently wrote in Esquire, the Beatles "made it not just OK but insanely desirable to be a stylish, successful, smartarse

British man." The representation of masculinity embodied in *Help!* is a key stepping stone to more obvious displays of gender fluidity that were to emerge in later decades.

The music journalist, Ian MacDonald, says the Beatles were critical to popular culture in the 1960s because of their global fame and the media interest in their activities. He argues that they were therefore a prism through which social changes were magnified and reflected.

Their first feature film, *A Hard Day's Night* (1964) had provided a global audience with the chance to see a mockumentary about a day in the life of the Beatles at the height of Beatlemania. Despite their exuberance, feminised appearance and a number of queer moments (such as Lennon batting his eyelids and saying "give us a kiss" to a bowler hatted gent in a railway carriage), the film had much in common with the new-wave kitchen sink dramas of the early 1960s. It presented the most famous men on the planet as trapped by their day job; work central to their male identity.

But *Help!* sees them as men at play, in a technicolour international travelogue ranging from London to the Bahamas. Here it is not work but style, upward mobility and independent exotic living that become central to their identity as 60s Englishmen. There is also no central romantic plot, a significant break with cinematic convention.

Nonsense: Described by Chris Hutchins in his NME review at the time as "100 minutes of nonsense", the plot of *Help!* revolves around the attempt of a rogue Eastern religious sect to retrieve a sacrificial ring sent to Ringo by a fan. Yes, it's silly.

The beginning of the film emphasises a shift from reality to fantasy. First the Beatles are seen in black and white, wearing black roll-neck sweaters and Beatle boots in what looks like an outtake from *A Hard Day's Night*. The next time they appear, they're in colour. Like Dorothy in *The Wizard of Oz*, they have travelled from the black and white "reality" of Kansas (read Liverpool) to the Technicolour fantasy world of Oz (read pot-fuelled swinging London, 1965). Director Dick Lester brings a style over substance fantasy approach which pre-empts other key 60s texts, such as *Batman* and *The Avengers*, that bring the extraordinary to the ordinary.

This ordinary yet extraordinary nature of the Beatles is established in a memorable early scene where they arrive in a limousine in a terraced street and walk up to the doors of four adjoining terraced houses. As they step through four separate front doors, they enter one large communal room filled with contemporary designer furniture.

This transition is another that mirrors the shift from the black and white reality of 1964 to the technicolour hyperreality of 1965. It is also reflective of the potentially different lifestyle opening up for men in the mid 1960s. The house is a fantasy world where expectations created by the outside are subverted by the inside view. They are men reclaiming the indoors, independent and homosocial.

Metrosexual prototypes: Bearing this in mind, Mark Simpson's 1994 "identification" of the metrosexual clearly has its roots firmly in the mid 1960s. Simpson describes the typical metrosexual as a young man with money to spend, living in or within easy reach of the metropolis, who could be gay, straight or bisexual. The Beatles in *Help!* undoubtedly fit these criteria: they dramatize the increasing feminisation of men's visual appearance, characterised by increased hair length and an ever more dandified dress sense.

The clothes worn by the Beatles in *Help!* are a development of the mod style of the early 1960s. Suits are worn with coloured roll-neck sweaters, coloured shirts begin to be introduced along with materials such as corduroy and denim and the addition of capes and hats. A scene where they are seen recording on Salisbury Plain wearing a camped-up version of military attire is just one example from the film where they are juxtaposed with traditional sartorial symbols of masculinity and subvert them.

Two years after *Help!* The Beatles would push the boundaries of male attire and masculine possibilities still further, frolicking in the psychedelic foliage of the *Magical Mystery Tour*. But the initial thrust of change is nowhere better depicted than in *Help!*, a film that encouraged nothing less than the re-imagination of the Englishman.

∾

"The Beatles, Help! And the Creation of the Modern British Man,"
Martin King. Originally published on The Conversation.

[FOURTEEN]

Pandemonium at Shea

By Michael J. Fensom

The people who were there on that summer night knew by the massive size of the crowd and the sheer electricity in the air that they were seeing history in the making. No band had ever attempted a stadium concert before. Bruce Morrow of WABC Radio remembers that night at New York's Shea Stadium. —L.M.

∾

A few minutes past 9 on the evening of Aug. 15, 1965, Bruce Morrow was in the dugout alongside third base at Shea Stadium. The sun had set, but the late summer heat lingered and stifled, intensifying the uneasiness of the moment.

John Lennon, in a beige jacket, unbuttoned, and with a Rickenbacker 325 six-string tucked under his right arm, turned to Morrow. "Cousin, is this going to be all right?" Lennon asked, addressing Morrow like the thousands who phoned "Cousin Brucie" at New York's WABC radio each week to request he play the Beatles.

In 1965, The Beatles—Lennon, Paul McCartney, George Harrison and Ringo Starr—were the biggest rock 'n' roll band in the world and already familiar with fame. Their popularity was so great that the 1964 mockumentary A *Hard Day's Night* opened with hundreds of frothing fans chasing the band through the streets of London.

But 50 years ago this month, 55,600 people filled Shea Stadium, unified in a hysterical, unceasing chorus of shrieks and shouts. A string of New York City police—some with their index fingers stuck in their ears—created a human rope around the perimeter of the stadium's baseball field.

Three rows of wooden barricades and some chicken wire penned in the stage, a seemingly light deterrent should the frenzied thousands surge from the stands. Neither the Beatles nor anyone else were sure what would happen once the band emerged. A rock concert had never been held in a stadium before, and there was no one to yell, "Cut!"

Morrow scanned the tense scene in the makeshift bunker. Harrison was alone in a corner, maybe praying. Ed Sullivan, who, with the then-29-year-old Morrow, would bring the Beatles to the stage, was wide-eyed and sweating. A sign on the wall read "No Spitting," not a problem considering the surrounding dry-mouth anxiety.

"I was scared, too," Morrow recalls. "If that tide would have broken, it would have been disaster. I don't think there has ever been so many people contained in that sort of area."

Nonetheless, he reassured Lennon: "What you're hearing out there is emotion. It's love. All these people want to do is be here with you in the space."

"I hope they can hear us," Lennon replied.

When the Beatles stepped onto the infield grass at 9:17, ascended the steps to the stage positioned above second base and strummed the opening notes of "Twist and Shout," it marked the peak of Beatlemania. In five years, they would be through, disbanded without ever again sharing such an epic moment on stage with their fans.

The show revolutionized the music industry by demonstrating the commercial viability of a live concert on such a grand scale.

And for those at Shea Stadium that night, the Beatles' 12-song, half-hour set provided a tingling surge of youthful animation that hasn't been topped.

Lennon, who was noticeably giddy throughout the concert, recalled a decade later, "I saw the top of the mountain when we were at Shea."

"It's something I've never again experienced," says Morrow. In a studio at SiriusXM radio in New York, where he hosts "Cruisin' with Cousin Brucie" on Wednesdays, from 5 to 9 p.m. (repeated throughout the week), on Channel 6, Morrow has a photograph of himself interviewing the Beatles in 1965 at the Warwick Hotel.

The idea to play Shea Stadium was a bet laid down by New York promoter Sid Bernstein. The Beatles had played two shows at Carnegie Hall a year earlier, but with their popularity at its height, Bernstein, ever the booster, wanted to raise the stakes. He booked the sparkling new stadium in Queens to begin the Beatles' 1965 North American tour and when manager Brian Epstein doubted the band could sell out a stadium that large, with tickets going between $4.50 and $5.75, Bernstein guaranteed he would buy back every unsold seat for $10.

As the Beatles surged in Europe, Capitol Records was initially reluctant to release their singles in the United States. But in the final days of 1963, when the young voices of Lennon, McCartney and Harrison hit the radio waves in three-part harmony singing "I Want to Hold Your Hand," they were an instant hit.

Mark Lapidos, who, in 1974, founded The Fest for Beatles Fans, a biannual weekend gathering for thousands of Beatles devotees, recalls hearing that single one day after school in early January 1964 as a 16-year-old growing up in River Edge.

"I thought, 'What a strange name for a band.' The next day, I came home from school, a Tuesday, and the song was No. 1 on WABC," Lapidos says. "The music jumped off the grooves."

The core of the Beatles' popularity was among teenagers like Lapidos. Kids in search of a music genre of their own, at a time when the music industry was, as Morrow characterizes it, "very tired." In addition to the fresh-sounding songs, young girls were attracted to the band's Scouse accents and good looks. Teenage boys picked up guitars and tried imitating the group's unknotted style. Adults, initially wary of the Beatles' mop-top haircuts, eventually came to embrace the band's melodic music.

Morrow says it was not uncommon to spin "I Want to Hold Your Hand" eight times in succession on WABC, then the region's biggest Top 40 station. Audiences in New York and New Jersey couldn't get enough of the Beatles, and the area's wholesale embrace made the show at Shea Stadium a possibility.

"New Jersey was a major market attached to New York that helped build this thrust to hyper-popularity," says Morrow, who, in 2010, received an honorary Doctor of Letters degree from Montclair State University.

Morrow watched the Beatles' performance looking up at the stage from home plate, as if an umpire, and couldn't hear a note. (Morrow says he finally heard a recording of the show earlier this year.) But as soon as the Beatles' set concluded with "I'm Down," Morrow asked police to whisk him through the tunnels underneath the Shea stands to his car. Before the stadium unpacked, Morrow was driving home to Manhattan and remembers noticing, for the first time all night, that he was sweating.

When he arrived home, he sat down at his desk, took a deep breath and became nauseous.

"My body realized what I had just been through," Morrow says. "Anyone I've talked to since that day, who was there, can't forget details of that day and the emotions that they felt. That's how important it was sociologically to our lives."

～

[FIFTEEN]

Hair, Drugs and Rock and Roll

By Steven D. Stark

1965-66 was an extremely formative time for the Beatles. Writer and cultural commentator Steven D. Stark details how the non-stop work schedule and overbearing commercialism brought on by their immense success made the Beatles retreat inward. Drugs, new relationships, and spiritual soul-searching led the boys to develop new outlooks on life that would manifest in the increasingly innovative music of their later years. The drug use and personal evolution not only changed their music—it had profound impact on the broad counterculture of which they became the chief exponents. —L.M.

⌒

Three major attributes helped define the emerging youth culture of the mid-sixties. Two of these—the maturing sensibility of rock music and the move to personal freedom symbolized by long hair—wouldn't have happened without the Beatles. The third—the ubiquitous use of drugs—the Beatles wouldn't have happened without. Because the Beatles were so associated with these three developments, when a backlash began to develop against them and what they represented, there was a backlash against the Beatles.

The Beatles, said George Martin, "were more brilliant than they realized and it would have happened without drugs." But he was wrong: Though few at the time knew the extent of their drug use, drugs had fueled the Beatles almost from the beginning and refashioned the group even before those same substances, with the band's implicit endorsement, remade the wider youth culture. In fact, when the *Beatles Monthly Book*, their unofficial fan magazine, published its last issue in December 1969, the publisher stepped away from the magazine's usually rapturous tone to blast the group for the way it had encouraged drug use among the young.

"Marijuana started to find its way into everything we did," said Paul. "It colored our perception and we started to realize there weren't as many barriers as we thought."

Soon it would do the same for millions. More than any other factor, drugs provided the foundation for the sixties counterculture. "In many ways, the counterculture was about altered states of consciousness, which really meant drugs," said Robin Richman, who reported on the era for *Life* magazine. "That led to a number of the changes in the sixties."

Drugs provided the backdrop for the era, even for those who chose not to take them. The influence of marijuana and psychedelics was everywhere. The drug-inspired emphasis on those "altered states of consciousness" helped fuel the interest in alternative forms of religion. The way drugs heightened sensation and helped loosen the bounds of morality were factors in stoking the sexual revolution.

Alcohol—the drug of choice of previous generations—was the source of pub fights and lonely idylls on bar stools, while tending to make imbibers more aggressive and raucous. In contrast, marijuana and the more popular psychedelic drugs of the sixties tended to reduce aggression, helping to cement the notion of peace as a key element in the growing counterculture.

"Drugs helped bring it all about," said Maggie McGivern, Paul's girlfriend later in the decade. "But bloody hell, it worked."

In their use of drugs, the Beatles were hardly alone in the music community. Drugs have been an important engine of popular music, producing changes in style based on the drug choice at the moment.

In a way, it is possible to tell the story of the group's music through the drugs they were on at various times. The Beatles had begun in Liverpool and Hamburg as an alcohol- and amphetamine-driven band, and that didn't change during their first year of world fame. "They were always drinking," remembered photographer Harry Benson, with the usual drinks of choice being Scotch and Coke or Scotch and lemonade. To keep going, the band members were also on Dexedrine or Preludin, colloquially called "Purple Hearts," also popular among college students who need to stay up all night studying. George remembered that when they flew from England to Hong Kong in mid-1964 the Preludins and alcohol made a long trip seem like it had taken ten minutes.

"They were all on Purple Hearts in the early sixties," said journalist Chris Hutchins, who hung out with the group. "Those drugs make you more promiscuous, more creative, more excited—you want to do more, talk more." That sense of acceleration, of course, had found its way into much of the Beatles' early music even if observers didn't know its well-spring. (The Beatles seemed to play "Roll Over Beethoven" twice as fast as Chuck Berry did.)

One associate who shared the group's predilection for uppers was manager Brian Epstein. "I discovered far more about amphetamines around Eppie than I ever learned around John Lennon," Hutchins said. "Eppie was constantly hopped up. We would go out to eat at the finest fish restaurant in London and he'd order a bottle of the best wine and the first thing he'd do is swallow pills. 'Here's five for you and five for me,' he'd say. Then he'd never touch his food."

Many of their compatriots were doing the same thing. "It should have been called 'Speeding London,'" said Harry Shapiro, author of a history of drugs and popular music. Andy Warhol described a similar phenomenon across the Atlantic. "I could never finally figure out if more things happened in the sixties because there was more awake time for them to happen (since so many people were on amphetamine) or if people started taking amphetamine because there were so many things to do that they needed to have more awake time to do them in," he said. "It was probably both."

Like so much else in the Beatles story, there is disagreement about when the Beatles were first introduced to marijuana. What is clear, however, is that toking up with influential older rival Bob Dylan in New York on their '64 summer tour of the U.S. launched the group into marijuana nirvana. Passing around a joint, the group put wet towels under the door of their New York hotel room, hoping to conceal the smell.

From that point on, though their fans didn't know it at first, all four Beatles were consistently stoned on marijuana—and soon on more—for much of the rest of their existence. "We believed in cannabis as a way of life," said Derek Taylor.

Marijuana had been in vogue among jazz musicians for decades and the Beats had endorsed its properties as well. But its widespread popularity in the 1960s greatly expanded its influence. In the words of one record executive, marijuana "worked wonders in the music industry . . . It gave musicians that sense of heightened awareness and produced classic hits."

What made music in the sixties unique, of course, is that the use of illicit drugs soon became so widespread that it was assumed (often correctly) that the audience was on the same drugs as the musicians. Much of the music of the period was produced with this thought in mind (which is why so much of it is unlistenable today).

"Over time there had been a gradual disengagement of young people from the adult culture," said Erich Goode, a sociology professor who has written frequently about the history of drug use. "That youth culture was more adventurous, risk-taking, and anti-establishment. The use of marijuana fit in with all of those things and had the advantage of being fun to use too. Once it started in earnest, it spread like wildfire."

Soon virtually everyone seemed to be smoking grass even though it was illegal—at concerts, political rallies, parties, and at home, helping to create the sense of a persecuted rebellious community that was essential to the zeitgeist of the youth culture. Landon Jones later wrote that if the popularity of this sacrament could be reflected in the number of words it added to the English language, there was little that could match the popularity of pot or grass, reefer, hash, dope, Mary Jane, J's, or weed which could cause one to be zoned out, stoned, down, turned on, or zonked.

"For a counterculture beginning to question hectic aggressiveness of the culture at large, marijuana was the perfect antidote: It made the user more introspective and passive," said Keith Stroup, an attorney and founder of the National Organization for the Reform of Marijuana Laws.

It was also a good fit for the Beatles. Even before they had discovered the drug, the adjectives people often used to describe the group were "happy" and "nonthreatening"—adjectives similar to the ones frequently invoked to describe the drug's effects on users. The Rolling Stones and marijuana never quite seemed to fit together; grass and the Beatles were a match made in Heaven.

At first marijuana probably changed John—who once said, "I've always needed a drug to survive" —more than the others.

"John knew he had a problem when he drank," said Dan Richter, his aide and friend in the late sixties. "People who have trouble controlling their emotions and have repressed feelings often turn to drugs. As did John."

It worked. Marianne Faithfull said that when he stopped drinking he became much less aggressive.

By the beginning of 1965, John later admitted, he was smoking marijuana for breakfast, and George and Ringo were no strangers to the drug either. Paul, though he would avoid acid for the most part, was also no slouch in the marijuana department. One member of the inner circle later recalled that when Paul first got together with his future wife, Linda Eastman, one of her trademarks was that she traveled around with virtually the biggest bag of marijuana anyone had ever seen.

The first effects of the Beatles' new use of grass had already become apparent to insiders by the end of 1964, when their annual Christmas message to their fans was marked by chronic giggling. Their dope smoking revealed itself even more during the filming of their second movie, *Help!*, shot early in 1965. The Beatles were often so high during the filming that it was hard to get work done. One day in May, director Lester tried to film a short scene outside Buckingham Palace more than twenty times and finally had to quit. "They would break up and giggle and whack each other with their elbows," said one American reporter on the scene. "The Beatles were just too high to continue shooting."

By mid-1965, the drug use was affecting their music. The changes "really began when Bob Dylan gave marijuana to the Beatles and the Beatles' music changed, there's no doubt about it," said Derek Taylor.

After that first meeting, Dylan became more like the Beatles and the Beatles more like him. Within a year, Dylan had "gone electric" at the Newport Folk Festival and on his albums—trading in his folk sound for the more cutting edge of the electric guitar and entering the higher reaches of the rock charts for the first time with "Like a Rolling Stone."

The Beatles were similarly transformed. "I've never been so excited about meeting any other musician before," John had said prior to that initial encounter. Up until that point, the lyrics of Beatles songs had not been particularly sophisticated. That was in sharp contrast to folk music and the work of Dylan, who had said that "the words are just as important as the music; there would be no music without the words."

When Dylan moved into rock, he brought other folkies along as well, like the Lovin' Spoonful and the Mamas and the Papas. Yet he didn't have the mass popularity the Beatles enjoyed. When the Beatles' music became more intellectual and socially responsive, it affected *everybody*. "The Beatles came along and that was pretty much it," said Darby Slick of the Great Society band in San Francisco. "Folk music just went instantly into the dumper."

By 1965, Americans were already familiar with the notion that youth were on the march, inspired by the moral clarity of the civil rights movement. Student protesters seemed to be everywhere—as Freedom Riders in the South in 1961, as volunteers at Freedom Summer in the same region in 1964, and later that same year at Berkeley as part of the Free Speech Movement. Though rock had always been associated with rebellion, folk music was, of course, the traditional music of political protest. When folk and rock began to converge—thanks in large part to both the Beatles and Dylan—rock began to acquire much of the edge and relevance that folk had carried in American culture, even if the lyrics of the new genre weren't nearly as pointedly political as those of folk music had been. (Reflecting the change, rock and roll now tended to be described a bit more seriously as just "rock.")

This meant, too, that rock music could become more intellectual. Because of their background the Beatles had always possessed artistic aspirations unusual for rock musicians. "Before the Beatles, rock had a lot of id but not much ego," said Neal Gabler, a cultural historian. "Around this time the Beatles did something terribly unusual and difficult: They took the serious questions usually asked in high culture and brought them into popular culture."

From mid-1965 on, the trend in rock toward articulating a broader dissatisfaction with society was obvious. Besides Dylan's "Like a Rolling Stone," the charts soon included folklike protest songs like Barry McGuire's "Eve of Destruction" ("You're old enough to kill, but not for voting!"), Donovan's "Catch the Wind," and Simon and Garfunkel's "The Sounds of Silence." In the words of writer Jacob Weisberg, a genre which began as "a moan about parental authority" was now on its way "to a questioning of institutional and governmental power." While rock and roll had traditionally reflected its teen buyers in a preoccupation with relationships and sex, that too was shifting. Within a few years, one scholar would find the percentage of the genre's songs not dealing with love and courtship in some form up to about a third from close to zero.

Soon, there was widespread belief, naive in retrospect but understandably powerful, that the sheer energy and generational impetus of rock could transform the world. Later in the decade the San Francisco journalist Ralph Gleason wrote, "I am convinced that rock 'n' roll in its total manifestations will cause one [a government] to fall," and millions believed him. "Out of it will come the programs. Out of it will come the plans," he wrote.

"It was a political statement," said Joe Boyd, cofounder of the UFO rock club in London, "to get stoned and listen to somebody improvise on an Indian modal scale for twenty minutes with an electric group playing around him."

"Pop music is the beginning," said Donovan. "Fashion will change, architecture, eating, everything because we want it a certain way and we're going to do it."

That unshakable commitment to personal freedom as enunciated by Donovan would soon be at the core of the embryonic counterculture in its struggle with "the establishment." By 1966, the mood had spread virtually worldwide. A dispute in Communist East Germany over whether youth should be allowed to listen to the Beatles and other rock groups was creating, according to the *New York Times*, "the greatest internal turmoil in East Germany since the Berlin Wall was erected." The authorities finally gave up: "East Germany Commies Surrender to Beatles," read the headline in *Variety*. "Battle Was Lost Anyway."

"The Beatles would cultivate a generation of freedom-loving people throughout this country that covers one-sixth of the Earth," wrote Mikhail Safonov years later about the band's effect in the Soviet Union. "Without that love of freedom, the fall of totalitarianism would have been impossible, however bankrupt economically the communist regime may have been."

Yet the first important battle in many places wasn't over music. Beauty may be only skin deep, but how one looked began to take on major cultural and political significance. The Beatles directly inspired this struggle. Though conflicts over hair length may seem trivial today, at the time they took on the cast and language of other fights for individual freedom.

"Yes my hair is long and I haven't shaved in days," sang a folksinger at a Berkeley demonstration. "But I'm fighting for my freedom while clean-cut kids look the other way."

"The issue of hair," said fan Marcy Lanza, "was viewed in the context of the civil rights movement. To us, it was about the same issue—freedom."

Up until this point, the main focus of the group's cultural impact had been on girls—the instigators of Beatlemania. Now it switched to the other sex as the cultural prospects of liberation began to tempt boys as well.

For a long time, of course, long hair on boys was simply called a "Beatle haircut." Only the year before, in 1964, the group's hair had been shorter and, though nontraditional, still considered by many to be more strange than threatening. As their locks steadily grew longer, however—and with it the hair of practically every member of a white rock band—the message changed and millions followed. The length of hair on men now became the preeminent symbol of whether one was part of the youth revolt or not. The rebellion was easy to accomplish: All you had to do was stop going to the barber.

"Hair," read *Amy Vanderbilt's Book of Etiquette*, "because it is so obvious, easy, and cheap to manipulate and color, has always been a frontline symbol of teenage rebellion."

The first signs of generational warfare within families, schools, and communities now often centered on hair length; many of the cases litigating the extent to which authorities could force boys to cut it reached the federal courts. In fact, long hair soon came to represent a multitude of Utopian possibilities, so much so that when the creators of a musical several years later wanted to describe the whole sensibility of the new age they simply entitled it *Hair*.

Because they were older, there wasn't much authorities could do about college students, who in the wake of the Berkeley Free Speech Movement in 1964 began organizing across the country to get rid of campus hair and dress codes and—while they were at it—parietal hours dictating when the other sex could visit dorm rooms.

The real struggle was with younger teens in high schools, where the example of the college protests trickled down. "Big Sprout-Out of Male Mop Tops" read the headline of a story in *Life* magazine in the summer of '65 that related how teenage boys across the country were refusing to toe the line in school and get their hair cut. One analyst complained that "a Beatle-type hair style can be as frightening a symbol as a switchblade." As Grace Palladino has documented in her book, *Teenagers*, the issue was covered intensely by the media—especially the youth press in publications such as America's *Senior Scholastic* and *Seventeen*. These were hardly radical organs, but as style arbiters, some of these magazines picked up the cry that youth should be able to fashion their hair and dress any way they wanted.

Soon rigid, gender-bound modes of appearance and behavior began to break down among the young. "Are You a Boy or Are You a Girl?" sang the Barbarians. Not only was hair getting longer, but men (the Beatles included) began to wear beads, necklaces, and bright, embroidered clothes made of unusual fabric. Literary critic Leslie Fiedler commented on how the new rising spirit of collectivism was essentially a feminine notion—a revolt against the competitive male individualism that dominated American culture.

Meanwhile, the Beatles' second movie was released in the summer of '65. Even without the drug factor, the film was not destined to be the artistic success that *A Hard Day's Night* had been. Originally *Help!* was going to be something of a sequel to the first film (Lester wanted to call it *Beatles 2*), with a plot concerning a man (Ringo) who wakes up one day, decides he can't stand the pressure of fame, and hires a hit man to kill himself. Then he changes his mind and tries to find the hit man to call it off. The idea had some possibilities with its connection to the way the Beatles were feeling about the constrictions of celebrityhood. Unfortunately, Lester discovered that a film with a similar story line was already in production.

Stuck for a plot, Lester settled on a James Bond-type spoof—a kind of cinematic comic book that Lester said was exploring the "correlation between pop music, pop art, and a pop movie." At another moment, Lester told reporters, "You'll find nothing new about *Help!* There's not one bit of insight into the social phenomenon of our times."

Nevertheless, like its predecessor, the film continued the Beatles' conversation with their fans, giving their audience something to go see again and again in the summer of '65. (A new Saturday morning Beatle cartoon series in the U.S., licensed without their artistic control, extended the dialogue to the under-ten set beginning that September.) And with the release of the *Help!* LP that summer, the Beatles continued their move in a new folk-oriented Dylanesque direction. The lyrics became sharper and more autobiographical—a trend that had accelerated when journalist Maureen Cleave of London's *Evening Standard* had told John he should start writing songs with more than just one-syllable words. (It was also Cleave who had suggested a change in "A Hard Day's Night," after Lennon had originally written "When I get home to you, I find my tiredness is through.")

On *Help!* the Beatles also developed a gentler, more acoustic sound on songs such as "You've Got to Hide Your Love Away" and "Yesterday." It became more difficult to dance to their songs because of the slower tempo. (John had written "Help!" as an even slower tune, but to his eternal displeasure, producer George Martin made him speed it up to have more commercial appeal.)

Thanks in large part to Martin, who brought a classical sensibility to rock music, the Beatles also began using outside musicians—a flautist on "You've Got to Hide Your Love Away" and a string quartet on "Yesterday." In fact, while today's critics tend to see the early link between Dylan and the Beatles mostly in John's autobiographical songs, at the time it tended to be Paul's "Yesterday" that struck critics as Dylanesque because it involved a singer accompanied only by a guitar (plus the classical musicians suggested by Martin).

"Paul goes it alone on a Dylan-styled piece of material," wrote *Billboard* in its review.

"Yesterday"—perhaps the Beatles' best-known tune—was a shock in rock at the time. It remains one of the most popular songs ever written, covered by other artists over 2,500 times. Yet there's evidence that its singularity was a point of contention among the Beatles. It was the first time the Beatles had released a song that didn't feature the entire group. Moreover, until then John had been controlling much of the group's output and he appeared to resent Paul's success with a song that appealed to adults as much as to young rockers. "What a load of bloody crap!" John said when he heard the tune, to which George added within hearing distance, Paul "thinks he's Beethoven."

It could hardly have pleased lead guitarist George either that on "Ticket to Ride," released as a single in the spring of '65, Paul took over Harrison's guitar duties, presumably because he thought he could do it better. Within a few months, a studio producer said, "The clash between John and Paul was becoming obvious. Also, George was having to put up with a lot from Paul. . . . As far as Paul was concerned, George could do no right." Meanwhile John was reportedly miffed that Martin, presumably at Paul's instigation, had asked Brian Epstein if McCartney could get sole or primary credit for "Yesterday," rather than the usual "Lennon-McCartney" notation. Epstein said no. (McCartney would obsess over this for decades, and forty years later he was still fighting with Yoko Ono over who should get primary credit for the song.) None of these spats were apparent to the public at the time.

What didn't change on *Help!* was John's attitude to women. On "You're Gonna Lose That Girl" he repeated the unusual-for-rock theme from "She Loves You" that those who treat women badly deserve to lose their affection. And on "Ticket to Ride," he sung of passively sitting by while his woman deserted him yet again, repeating the preoccupation that had plunged him since childhood.

Meanwhile the Beatles continued to tour. They hit France, Italy, and Spain that summer of '65, where, to their surprise, their shows didn't sell out even though Paul tried to introduce the songs in the native language of the country they were visiting. In December, they did nine concerts in their homeland. In between, in August, they headed to the U.S. and Canada again, where they did sixteen shows in ten venues (plus *The Ed Sullivan Show*) in eighteen days.

What was more striking than the pace of this 1965 return tour was its scope. The Beatles began appearing in large stadiums, opening the tour before almost fifty-six thousand fans at Shea Stadium in New York. This was the beginning of "stadium rock," and apparently the size of the screaming mobs began to alarm the Beatles. That show, Ringo remembered, made John "crazy."

Mick Jagger, who loved attention and was in the crowd, had a similar reaction. "It's frightening!" he said.

When the Beatles came off the road late that summer of '65, they tentatively decided that they had to stop touring soon, though no one could yet envision an alternative. From September 1965 until the following May the Beatles rarely played a live show. Capturing the difference in their style between the touring period and the new one to come—which eventually encompassed everything from their music, to the drugs they were on, to their sensibility—Tony Barrow called the periods the "Old and New Testament eras."

The transformation marked yet another dividing line. Though the Beatles had toyed with the concept of moving away from live performances ever since they had first entered a recording studio three years earlier, the group now began creating music to be heard only on record rather than in performance. "Coming into the studio was a refuge for them," said George Martin, and the group began staying past midnight, working on their records. "It was a time and place when nobody could get at them."

The Beatles also began to think of each album as a presentation in itself, like a film or a novel; within two years, LP sales, thanks to their example, eclipsed sales of singles for the first time.

"When I first started in the music business," said George Martin, "the ultimate aim for everybody was to try and re-create, on record, a live performance as accurately as possible. But then, we realized that we could do something other than that. In other words, the film doesn't just re-create the stage play. So, without being too pompous, we decided to go into another kind of art form, where we are devising something that couldn't be done any other way."

With Martin's help, the Beatles now began fashioning yet another new paradigm. Critic Paul Saltzman later called the Beatles "the first poets of technological culture." In the words of one scholar, "the quest for the illusion of reality, of bringing into the living room the sensation of being in a concert hall, was replaced with a new sonic world which could not actually exist, a pseudo-reality created in synthetic space." This new "pseudo-reality" also fit in well with the ethos of the emerging drug culture, which also aimed at exploring alternative visions of reality.

It took almost two years for the Beatles to perfect the model. The first transitional product of their new efforts was *Rubber Soul*, released in December 1965. "*Rubber Soul*, for me, is the beginning of my adult life," said Paul at the time. Not everyone loved this "adulthood": It was an album, wrote one commentator, that for the first time in the group's career "erred on the side of pretension rather than simplicity."

"Without a shadow of a doubt the Beatles' sound has matured," wrote the critic for the influential *New Musical Express* in reviewing *Rubber Soul*. "But unfortunately it also seems to have become a little subdued."

As with *Help!* earlier in the year, the Dylan-and marijuana-influenced tempo stayed slower as the words became more meaningful and more personal. ("*Rubber Soul* was the pot album," John later said.) The group introduced new instruments and sounds: a sitar on "Norwegian Wood (This Bird Has Flown)" and a guitar played to sound like a Greek bouzouki on "Girl." Romances were no longer boy meets girl and falls in love. At times, Paul and John told unconventional stories, as in "Norwegian Wood" about an illicit love affair gone astray, or "Girl," about a woman whose attitudes puzzle her lover, or "Drive My Car," a song they described as a comic short story. The "she" of earlier songs was now occasionally given a real name, as in "Michelle."

All this continued to be in contrast to what was going on elsewhere in rock. Though rock music was gradually becoming more political, it wasn't becoming feminized; in fact often the opposite. At around the same time the Beatles were recording *Rubber Soul*, the Rolling Stones were singing about not being able to get any satisfaction; Mick Jagger would soon be putting women under his thumb in hits that poured out "a psychotic flood of abuse against women," according to one author.

Dylan, the other patron saint of the new music, was scarcely a feminist either, though admittedly the relationships described in his songs were hardly the simple romances of traditional rock. "Dylan had contested many aspects of the dominant culture," analyst Paul Hodson later wrote, "but not its preferred styles of masculinity."

As some later noted, *Rubber Soul* was also striking—though few noticed this at the time—for the way in which Paul began to emerge as an engine of the group's product. His confidence appeared to be growing now that he was writing more—one reason that the songs on *Rubber Soul* were often more melody driven. As the Beatles began to do more work in the studio, Paul also started to take on a closer working role with George Martin, since the other three had less patience for the complexities of instrumentation and recording technique.

At around this time, John and George moved on to LSD, with Ringo slightly behind, creating another fissure with Paul. "They quite literally used to eat it like candy," said Pete Shotton of George and John. (Though acid wasn't for Paul—he probably took it fewer than a half dozen times—by the next year or so, he later admitted, he was into cocaine.)

The effect of their drug use on the culture, said one critic, was to clean up the image of psychedelics, making them more acceptable to their millions of followers. By the next year, Timothy Leary said, "I consider them [the Beatles] the four evangelists in the psychedelic movement."

The new drugs had different effects on each Beatle. For John, LSD stimulated the production of some of his most creative songs over the short term. Yet John's overuse of the drug—he once estimated he tripped more than a thousand times—eventually impaired his creative influence over the direction of the band. With John continually tripping, Paul started taking over more of the group's musical responsibilities. Though their work was still collective by anyone's description, Paul soon began writing a majority of the group's songs, which some speculate may have pushed John to escape by taking even more acid.

"In a way, like psychiatry, acid could undo a lot—it was *so* powerful you could just *see*," said George. "But I think we didn't really realize the extent to which John was screwed up."

"I can't disclose specifics, but in general I'll tell you this. LSD is the most devastating thing for mental health that ever existed," Arthur Janov, John's therapist in the late sixties and early seventies, told a reporter. "To this day, we see people who've been on LSD, and they have a completely different brain-wave pattern, as if their defences are totally broken down. It stays."

For George, acid was the impetus that sent him hurtling on a voyage of inquiry into Indian culture and music that eventually had a profound effect on all four Beatles. "It was like opening the door, really, and before that you didn't even know there was a door," he said. It wasn't a change everyone welcomed. Tony King, a friend, told reporter Steve Turner, the English rock writer, "When I first met George in 1963, he was Mr. Fun, Mr. Stay Out All Night. Then all of a sudden he found LSD and Indian religion and he became very serious. Things went from rather jolly weekends where we'd have a steak and a kidney pie and sit around giggling to these rather serious weekends where everyone walked around blissed out and talked about the meaning of the universe."

For the Beatles as a whole "it was only when LSD arrived, bringing an 'alternative' outlook for which inner freedom was more important than material success, that the pieces fell into place and the group's new direction became clear," wrote Ian McDonald later.

The single "Paperback Writer" and its flip side, "Rain," released in the late spring of 1966, continued the evolution of the New Testament Beatles as the songs landed in an America now preoccupied by LSD. In 1966, the drug was made illegal by Congress, and three powers in the magazine world—*Life*, *Newsweek*, and *Saturday Evening Post*—all devoted major stories to it. Influenced by John's "Nowhere Man," the group's first song not to deal with relationships in any form, Paul's "Paperback Writer" was both his first song to deviate from rock's fundamental obsession with romance and one of his few ministories, this one about a man trying to write a novel. While virtually all of the groups prior songs had been about relationships in some form before these singles, from now on fewer than one third would be. In fact, at this point John stopped writing traditional romantic songs altogether for two years, leaving that department solely to Paul.

The flip side of "Paperback Writer," John's "Rain," was, in critic Allan Kozinn's words, one of John's new songs that were primarily an "expression of attitude." The subject matter of the song revisited an old English preoccupation with the island's dank, dark conditions, much like the paintings of Turner.

As much as the lyrics, "Rain" forecast the sound of the new Beatles. As Mark Lewisohn later put it, "Rain" was "full of all the latest technological advancements: limiters, compressors, jangle boxes, Leslie speakers, ADT, tapes played backwards, machines deliberately running faster or slower than usual, and vari-speed vocals." John said he came up with the idea of an ending that played earlier parts of the song backward when he came home stoned one night and accidentally played a record from the studio topsy-turvy.

The new style caught their public unawares. "They have, to put it bluntly, goofed," wrote the critic for *London's Sunday Mirror* when reviewing the new single.

In fact, as observers later noted, half of the fourteen songs on the next album, *Revolver,* were drug songs of one form or another—not that this was apparent to most of the Beatles' public at the time. Paul's "Got to Get You into My Life," for example, was one of the best rocking love songs he ever wrote but it was evidently intended, at least in part, as a tribute to the power of drugs, not Jane Asher. He may have meant "Good Day Sunshine" to be nothing more than a paean to "being alive," but "knowing" hippies heard the lyrics and thought it, too, was about drugs.

Yet however one described the songs on *Revolver,* released in August 1966, they formed one of the most outstanding albums in the history of popular music. It was an album created by *artists,* with a panoply of styles and instrumentation unheard of in previous popular rock and roll. As critic Russell Reising later wrote, *Revolver* was the first album for the group that featured a song where the Beatles themselves played no instruments ("Eleanor Rigby"); the first song adapted from a literary source ("Tomorrow Never Knows"); the first to open with a composition by George ("Taxman"); and the first to feature a song in Indian style ("Love You To"). Thanks to the magic of the studio, the music and voices were continually accelerated or slowed; tape loops were spliced together to create strange sounds, and even Ringo joined in, putting a large woolen sweater inside his drum to distort its sound. "It seems now," wrote Richard Goldstein presciently in the *Village Voice* at the time, "that we will view this album in retrospect as a key work in the development of rock 'n' roll into an artistic pursuit." That "development," in turn, inspired the whole genre of rock to continue to evolve into something representing far more than simply adolescent rebellion. For better or worse, rock and roll and its countercultural disciples would now take themselves very seriously.

In keeping with this new approach, Paul's six songs on the album were several steps beyond anything he had written before—though far more traditional in a classical sense than John's. On "For No One," the principal instruments were a French horn and a piano; no other Beatles appeared except Ringo. "Good Day Sunshine"—a kind of music hall number—featured no lead guitar work. Neither did "Eleanor Rigby," another compelling Paul ministry, this one about an older unmarried woman, sung to the accompaniment of a string quartet arranged by George Martin. "Jane Asher had turned him on to Vivaldi," said John.

As for George Harrison, he had three songs on the album—more than he had produced for an LP so far. Without a collaborator, it had taken him longer to come into his own as a writer, and here, as in his songs over the past eighteen months, much of his work tended to reflect a rather sour attitude to love. As others have noted, Harrison's early "love songs" tended to be tinged with suspicion and defensiveness— "If I Needed Someone" (but, of course, I probably don't), or "You Like Me Too Much" (which is probably your problem, not mine). It was only when he began writing his own Indian-type music, beginning with "Love You To" on this album, that his tone changed.

John's five new songs on the album mostly celebrated the joys of escape—namely, sleeping or taking drugs. Though venerated by critics since, they were generally less accessible and not greeted at the time with the same kind of enthusiasm as Paul's compositions. (A British magazine poll of favorite *Revolver* tracks taken soon after the album's release found that fans placed only one of John's songs in the top five.) The first song John had written for the album, "Tomorrow Never Knows," began with the words from Timothy Leary's *The Psychedelic Experience*, which John would read while tripping. He asked George Martin to arrange the song as if four thousand monks were singing it perched on a mountain. With its use of strange percussion, backward tape loops, and John's voice run through a loudspeaker, it was among the most experimental tracks rock had yet seen.

There was another emerging theme on this album. It was a characteristic of acid that, in Jon Savage's words, it could make "you see the world anew, just like a child" and "cause another return to childhood." Maybe that's what Cynthia Lennon meant when she said that acid made John like a little boy again, escaping "from the imprisonment which fame had entailed."

There was a way in which the Beatles had often reminded observers of the very young. "They are like children in many ways," George Martin told Hunter Davies. "They love anything magical." In the words of another onlooker, they acted out the process of never growing up and their spirit of fun emphasized that connection. Writing later about their early look and sensibility, the novelist Alison Lurie described them as Christopher Robinesque, with their emphasis on the "childish impulses of noisy play and free impulse release." Their androgyny also reinforced memories of the time of life when the differences between boys and girls are often less pronounced and even blurred.

There is, in fact, an English tradition going back to the pastoralism of Wordsworth of worshipping childhood and creating adultless utopias full of Peter Pans, hobbits, or Alice in Wonderlands. It was an impulse that informed a growing revolution in style in Britain. "I saw no reason why childhood shouldn't last forever," said fashion developer Mary Quant in describing one of the notions that distinguished her work, characterized by big flowers and short, unshaped dresses.

"We've all of us grown up in a way that hasn't turned into a manly way," Paul said. "It's a childish way."

Whatever the causes, John now began writing about when he was a boy on songs such as "She Said She Said" and the upcoming "Strawberry Fields Forever," named after the orphanage near his home in Liverpool. On "Paperback Writer," the group sang "Frere Jacques" as the backing to the lead vocal. Since one member of the group always influenced the others, it was a notion that soon infatuated all the Beatles, whose new psychedelic world in song came to represent a kind of childhood Eden—an enchanting utopia for children where a new consciousness ruled. Given their influence, this emerging sensibility soon became part of the larger psychedelic counterculture, which, in one writer's words, now took "being childlike as a sign of mental health." A French writer called the new mood the "triumph of babydom over thought."

The song that best embodied this new mood on *Revolver* was "Yellow Submarine," with the lead sung by Ringo in his "everyman" role. Written by Paul, the family man who loved kids, the recording featured "magical" side effects like the sound of the ocean and included a brass band—a summer memory from the Beatles' childhoods in Britain, where bands play in parks constantly. It was easily singable, a trait evidenced by the fact that the Beatles brought a number of their friends into the studio to join the chorus. Its theme was, again, the joys of collectivism. With its colorful imagery of a magic kingdom to which reborn children could escape—like the stories in so much children's literature—it even became the source of a feature-length cartoon movie.

Soon this seemingly juvenile song had become much more.

Within months of the song's release, protesters at Berkeley—now militating against the Vietnam war—were singing the song together. Michael Rossman, a Free Speech activist, wrote in a leaflet:

> *The Yellow Submarine was first proposed by the Beatles, who taught us a new style of song. It was launched by hip pacifists in a New York harbor, and then led a peace parade of 10,000 down a New York Street. Last night we celebrated the growing fusion of head, heart, and hands; of hippies and activists; and our joy and confidence in our ability to care for and take care of ourselves and what is ours. And so we made a resolution which broke into song; and we adopt for today this unexpected symbol of our trust in our future, and of our longing for a place fit for us all to live in.*

Derek Taylor said something similar: "It's really like a kind of ark where, at least that's how I saw it, a Yellow Submarine is a symbol for some kind of vessel which would take us all to safety, but be that as it may, the message in that thing is that good can prevail over evil."

After *Revolver*—which took an almost unprecedented (for then) three months to record—the Beatles needed a rest. Instead, they were forced to hit the road in the summer of '66 for what would be the final time. Over three months, after playing one last UK concert, they headed to Germany, Japan, the Philippines, and lastly the U.S.

This tour confirmed their previous tentative decision to stop touring. They were unable to perform any of *Revolver*'s complicated songs in concert, or at least chose not to do so. For a group that prided itself on its professionalism, they were awful. Even Paul forgot the words to songs and John often played the wrong chords. They returned to Hamburg for their first time since their early days (the threat of paternity suits had kept them out until then, according to Brian's advisers), and saw Astrid for the first time in several years. "I felt sorry for them," she later wrote. "They had missed their youth in some way. I could see that in their eyes."

In Tokyo, the Beatles were scheduled to play at the Budokan arena for five shows in three days, and because it was considered something of a religious war shrine, there were numerous complaints. To head off trouble, the Japanese ordered thirty-five thousand police to protect the tour and there were three thousand policemen inside the concert hall. Meanwhile, the Beatles played on a raised stage, so anyone who broke through the numerous police blockades couldn't get at them.

At the next stop in Manila, in a celebrated incident, the Beatles failed to attend a party given by Imelda Marcos, the wife of the president. The result was that they were prevented from leaving the country until they had posted a tax bond. Their security force was withdrawn, leaving the four to run for their plane carrying their own luggage and equipment while fans attacked them. The authorities made their plane sit on the runway for hours. George, in particular, was afraid they might be busted.

But America, which had always greeted them with open arms, provided the real surprise at the end of that summer. In the year since they had last traveled there, the group had changed a lot as their drug use had moved them somewhat out of the middle American mainstream. But the country had changed too. In 1965, it had still been possible for most adults to view the Beatle-inspired youth movement and any unrest it engendered as something akin to the benign rambunctiousness always displayed by youngsters. With music and hair now becoming more radical political statements, however, that was no longer true.

Moreover, the Beatles were arriving in the middle of a summer of racial unrest as riots engulfed a number of American cities including Chicago, New York, and Cleveland. "America is not too settled at the moment," said Derek Taylor at the time. "There is much violence and the sun is burning out of the hard sky." With the Vietnam War escalating, antiwar rallies had also moved off the campuses and into the streets, becoming more militant. In response, Lew Hershey, the director of the selective service system, had announced that any student who illegally protested the draft could lose his deferment and be sent to war.

With generational and political battle lines hardening, a cultural backlash had developed that would foreshadow a major electoral backlash two years later, particularly in more conservative areas like the South. It was hard not to see that many had no use for the political evolution rock music was taking. In the spring of 1966, "The Ballad of the Green Berets"—as prowar a song as anyone could imagine—hit number 1 in America, and both Nancy and Frank Sinatra ("These Boots Are Made for Walking" and "Strangers in the Night" respectively) retook the top of the rock charts with pop that could have been hits five years earlier. Meanwhile, the Beatles' new, more subtle songs and image had little appeal for younger teenyboppers, who were about to go over en masse to groups such as the Monkees, a domesticated made-for-television version of the Fab Four, who premiered with their own show in NBC television that fall.

The Beatles were thus prime targets in the culture battles when they arrived in the U.S. in August. Matters got worse when, on the eve of their visit, the teen magazine *Datebook* published a Maureen Cleave interview with John Lennon from earlier in the year in which he had said the Beatles were now "more popular than Jesus." Few had noticed in largely irreligious England—in part because it was probably true—and, in fact, Lennon's remarks would hardly have been out of place in a *Time* magazine cover piece several months earlier that had asked the far more radical question "Is God Dead?"

But in the more religious American South, Lennon's remarks ignited an uproar. Preachers and law enforcement officers in the region had been railing for years about the pernicious effects of rock and roll. When native son Elvis and his southern cohorts had been leading the musical charge, however, it had been impossible to mount much of a counteroffensive. The Beatles, of course, were a different story. In response to the Lennon interview, there were radio-station sponsored bonfires throughout the region, burning Beatles records. The Ku Klux Klan and others picketed their concerts. A Pennsylvania state senator called for their concert to be canceled in his home state. When the group arrived in August 1966 for its first U.S. show in smoldering Chicago—where at about the same time Martin Luther King, Jr. was stoned by a hostile crowd while leading a march—Lennon was forced to apologize for his remarks, which was about the worst agony he could imagine.

Meanwhile the Beatles' new outlook was rubbing a lot of people the wrong way. In England it had been reported that the crowds to greet them were dwindling, and when the Beach Boys beat them out in a *New Musical Express* poll as to the best group of 1966, Don Short of the *Daily Mirror* wrote, "The decline and fall of the Beatles became official last night."

The group clashed with Capitol, its American label, as the company forced the band to change the cover of the album *Yesterday and Today* from an unsettling picture showing the foursome strewn with butchered meat and doll's heads into something more conventional. The backlash was also exacerbated by John—anxious to recover his "real self" after his apology—who now announced his support for those protesting the Vietnam War. Paul, too, was having to defend his remarks that "America is a lousy country where anyone who's black is called a nigger." What the group didn't realize—in fact no one did at the time—was that by being so vehemently attacked by "the establishment," the Beatles were solidifying their position as leaders of the counterculture.

Because of the drop in their popularity, most venues on the tour didn't sell out. This time, Shea Stadium didn't fill. In Seattle, half of the tickets for an afternoon show in a fifteen-thousand-seat indoor arena went unsold. Worse, the anger in the culture seemed to permeate the crowds that came to see them. Beatles fans had always been somewhat unruly, but this was a scary change in tone. In Cleveland, 2,500 fans invaded the field, stopping the concert. In Memphis, the group was hit by rotten fruit and the concert was delayed because of a bomb threat. In Los Angeles, there were continual clashes between fans and police during and after the concert with dozens of injuries. In New York, two girls threatened to jump from the twenty-second floor of a hotel unless they could see the group.

As George Harrison put it, the world had used the Beatles as an excuse to go mad and then blamed it on the group.

Death threats followed. The Beatles had eschewed the U.S. ticker tape parades because of memories of the JFK assassination, which had also prompted the unofficial guideline that the Beatles try to avoid appearing in front of an open window inside a hotel. Now they were frightened much of the time. Louise Harrison visited her brother in a hotel on the tour. "I remember looking at George as he stepped onto the fire escape," she said. "He turned and looked at me, and I always sort of got the impression that it was like the look that would be in the eye of a deer that was looking into the barrel of a gun." When a firecracker went off during their Memphis appearance, they looked around at each other to see who had gotten shot. Even Paul, the leading advocate for touring, was so upset that he began occasionally vomiting out of fear before performances. By the end of their last concert in San Francisco in late August, the group knew its touring days were over. "So now it's all over," George announced triumphantly when it was over. "I can stop pretending to be a Beatle now, people!"

For the first time in almost a decade, each Beatle decided to go his own way for several months. In September, George went to india with Pattie to study Indian culture and music, and there he also met a self-styled guru who called himself the Maharishi Mahesh Yogi. Paul went to Africa and then stayed in London, where his "self-education" in the burgeoning London underground continued and he wrote the score for a film, *The Family Way*. John went to Spain, where, with his hair cut to resounding publicity, he began filming *How I Won the War*, directed by Richard Lester. Ringo mostly hung out at home.

There was no formal announcement that touring had ended. But with members of the group scattering and refusing to announce the dates of future tours, the English press establishment concluded (with the American press following) that the group was slipping and probably breaking up for good. After all, the expected route for popular musicians at that time was to record songs quickly and then hit the road to publicize them.

"*Beatlemania* is at an end," wrote the *London Sunday Times*. "Beatles May Not Appear as Group Again," read the headline of the

Daily Telegraph. "At the Crossroads," wrote the *Daily Mirror,* "the Sad Dilemma of Four Very Talented Lads." Brian Epstein had continually to issue statements denying that the Beatles were a thing of the past.

Though they badly needed the rest, it was hardest on John, who without his mates seemed lost. "You seem to need them even more than they need you," his wife, Cynthia, told him. John had recounted to his friend Pete Shotton earlier that year that he had fallen to his knees one night and begged God to help him. "God, Jesus, or whoever the fuck you are—*wherever* you are—will you please, just once, just *tell* me what the hell I'm supposed to be doing?" He had said something similar to Maureen Cleave. "You see there's something else I'm going to do, something I must do," he said, "only I don't know what it is."

By the end of November, the foursome reunited in London. Apparently the synchronicity still existed: All four Beatles were now sporting similarly styled shorter haircuts. "We cannot stay in the same rut. We have got to move forward," Paul told a reporter, as if everything they had done so far counted for very little. They now began the demanding work that six months later would produce the album that would transform everything again: *Sgt. Pepper's Lonely Hearts Club Band.*

∽

[SIXTEEN]

George Martin: Master of the Beatles Sound

By Sasha Frere-Jones

Sasha-Frere Jones, a talented music-maker and prolific writer, discusses the legacy of legendary producer George Martin. —L.M.

∼

I was 7 years old the first time I read the word "producer" on an album. My parents, who owned mostly classical music LPs, had a handful of pop albums. They were all by the Beatles.

The album I listened to most was *Rubber Soul* because I liked the bit in "I'm Looking Through You" where a buzzing little guitar phrase appears right after the chorus. I didn't know I was looking for louder guitars, or noise, or punk rock. And I didn't know what a producer was. But there at the bottom of the back cover were the words "Produced by GEORGE MARTIN." I figured he had something to do with that funny, nasty guitar sound.

On Tuesday, George Martin died, at age 90. I've spent most of my life as a musician and a critic learning his work, forgetting his influence, avoiding him, relearning him and living in a world whose boundaries were his, for better and worse.

By the time I turned 21, I had already started my second band. We had just covered "Tomorrow Never Knows," a Beatles song I will still play without complaint, though there are dozens I simply can't because I've heard them so often I no longer recognize them as music. For my birthday, my parents gave me a newly published book by Mark Lewisohn called "The Beatles Recording Sessions: The Official Abbey Road Studio Notes, 1962-1970."

Like millions of other musicians after me, I read about all the tricks Martin, along with engineers Geoff Emerick and Ken Townsend, employed on "Tomorrow Never Knows." I was forever enlightened, puzzled and spoiled. There probably isn't a rock band that hasn't tried something stupid like swinging a microphone around someone while they sing or finding a Leslie cabinet—a box housing a speaker that rotates during playback—because they had the idea, loosely gleaned from Martin, that their unimpressive song would somehow get better if something was run through the Leslie and recorded on its own track.

The omnipresence of the Beatles and Martin's imagination was liberating and, eventually, oppressing. As a child, it was my entry into pop music. As a young man in a band, Martin's work shaped my approach to recording and led me to think of production as its own act, a process I could notice if I listened hard enough.

Everything that had seemed natural to me in recordings became suspect, not in a bad way, but in the way that Santa Claus is not real but it's still awfully nice that your parents bought you GI Joe with kung-fu grip. I would listen to recordings and try to figure out if something had been double-tracked or added after the fact.

As I came of age inside the independent rock community in the late '80s, there was a revolt against the sumptuous production values Martin and the Beatles enjoyed at Abbey Road. Recording songs live, fast and raw became its own virtue, which ironically mirrored the Beatles' early days, playing night after night in Hamburg and recording songs in single takes with no overdubs.

The Beatles are very hard to escape if you get it into your head that you are going to be in a band and go into a recording studio.

Martin's innovations become sort of a Steph Curry situation for people making multitrack recordings. At a certain point, when you haven't been able to conjure the perfectly liquid bass sound and beautifully altered vocal harmonies, Martin and his friends are no longer geniuses—they are your demons, your Mozart, your Voldemort.

No, you think, they can't have been that good. It was all that free studio time. It was just a perfect storm. And if you listen to enough solo Beatles albums you can talk yourself out of believing in them. It became cool, after all, to hate the Beatles. There was a rumor that, after Pussy Galore had covered all of the Rolling Stones' "Exile on Main Street," Sonic Youth was going to cover the Beatles "white" album, as sort of an Oedipal act. As Sonic Youth themselves wrote, "Kill Yr Idols."

Which is what happens when you finally go back to the Beatles albums. You can easily make the case that too many people have thought too much about what Martin and the Beatles achieved and not enough about, say, what Sly and Robbie did with Grace Jones. But unfortunately, Martin's work with the Beatles remains as uncanny and vivid as conventional wisdom holds it to be.

Even "simple" tracks like "No Reply" are nested eggs of perfect decisions in arrangement and mixing. Ringo Starr is a gentle presence until Lennon and McCartney sing "lie" together in the chorus—suddenly Starr's crash cymbal is enormous and frightening. The betrayal at the heart of the carefree song surges into view, and, hang on, there's a huge piano chord in here somewhere—was there always a piano in this song?

The Beatles are obviously the Beatles, and that certainly lifts your chances of becoming George Martin. But, then, would the Beatles be the Beatles if someone hadn't been there to turn the acrimonious songs into bossa nova Trojan horses, or turn Lennon's dissociative language into fairground anthems and backward bird sounds?

You don't even have to end up liking the Beatles. Pick a song on any album and turn everything else off. "Everybody's Got Something to Hide Except Me and My Monkey"—that still sounds so revved up, unnaturally alive.

Oh, they sped the tape up slightly during mix down. Thanks, George.

∾

[SEVENTEEN]

Mal Evans: The Beatles' Gentle Giant

Joe Rodgers

Malcom "Big Mal" Evans' story is a tragic one. He was with the band before they hit it big, and was wildly loyal to them until the end. Writer Joe Rodgers presents a detailed account of the bodyguard and road manager who never gave up on the Beatles dream. If there's a message to take away, it's that in our busy lives we can unwittingly neglect the needs of the people who truly care about us. —L.M.

∾

There are many contenders for the coveted title of "Fifth Beatle." Some qualify due to their brief yet influential period as a fifth musical component of the Beatles' early career. Candidates include Stu Sutcliffe (bass) and Pete Best (drums) and to a lesser degree Chas Newby, who temporarily replaced Sutcliffe on bass, and who declined John Lennon's request to join the group permanently in Hamburg in favour of returning to University.

Others qualify due to their business relationship with the group, Brian Epstein and Neil Aspinall spring to mind. Then you have production candidates: Geoff Emerick, Norman Smith and of course "Fifth Beatle" extraordinaire, George Martin. There is one candidate however who fits almost all criteria as "Fifth Beatle", and who spent more time with the group than possibly anyone else in their short professional career. Road manager, bouncer, minder, nursemaid, travelling companion, loyal friend, session musician, talent scout, producer and general dogsbody: step forward, Mr. Fixit, otherwise known as Mal Evans.

Born in 1935, Malcolm Evans was already married with a young family, a mortgage and a steady job as a communications engineer with the Post Office when he stumbled into a lunchtime Beatles session in 1962, altering his fate forever. After quickly befriending the group, George Harrison recommended Evans to Cavern owner Ray McFall as a bouncer at the chaotic underground entrance of the busy Liverpool music venue. This was a job that fit naturally with his calm demeanour and intimidating 6'6" hulking frame. In August 1962, just before Ringo Starr replaced Best and the group's career began to take off, Evans was hired by Brian Epstein to assist Aspinall in roadie duties. He soon became the default van driver, the man who patiently set up the group's backline equipment, tested it, stood by prepared for all disasters, and packed the van up again after the show had ended.

As Beatlemania emerged, Evans fulfilled a pivotal role beyond stage duties by serving as the royal guard, protecting the group from hordes of fans while also performing the discrete role of minister of selection for female companionship. In other words, Evans would be sent out from hotel rooms to find suitable groupies to party with the boys. Evans has the unique distinction of being present at every Beatles concert from the time he started working with them. From the ballrooms and clubs of early 1960s Britain to the baseball stadiums and orchestral bowls of the world's finest cities, if there was a fly on the wall, it was Mal Evans.

It was Evans who punched out a cracked windscreen on a freezing motorway and drove hundreds of miles through the night into howling winds while the group drank whiskey and huddled for warmth in the back. Evans was also frog-marched off the plane alongside Epstein in Manila, and punched by crowds when the Beatles came close to being lynched by a mob in 1966. His duties on the road brought him into close personal contact with the group, and Evans maintained a relationship and trust with all four Beatles which perhaps extended beyond that of their own wives and girlfriends.

He seemed to have enjoyed a particularly close relationship with both Lennon and Paul McCartney. He accompanied McCartney on a European road trip and African safari during the group's career hiatus after ceasing touring in 1966, and he was also known to serve as the group's watchdog when they were dropping acid. As they "turned on", Evans would remain with them to ensure their trips did not go bad or end in disaster.

This relationship was, however, almost completely one-sided. Although Evans was an insider on the rollercoaster that was Beatlemania, he was also often subjected to verbal abuse, becoming the scapegoat for anything that went wrong during a gig. He was subjected to Lennon's wrath many times, particularly for the theft of his beloved Gibson J160E acoustic guitar after a Christmas show in 1963. His role in the group's circle was somewhat accurately portrayed in the 1964 film *A Hard Day's Night* by the roadie character Shake. Harrison's line "Shake, where's me other boot? And would you get us some tea while you're there" seemed to echo Lennon's supposed trademark bark in Evans' direction: "Mal, Socks!"

Evans not only appears in *A Hard Day's Night* himself (carrying a cello down a hallway), but he has the distinction of appearing in every Beatles film, *Yellow Submarine* excepted. He appeared as a lost long-distance swimmer (*Help!*), a magician (*Magical Mystery Tour*), and several times as himself (*Let it Be*).

In addition to movie cameos, Evans also appears on several Beatles recordings despite being unable to play an instrument. The impressive run of credits include "You Won't See Me" (organ, single note), "Yellow Submarine" (bass drum and vocals), "A Day In The

Life" (ending piano, clock, and counting voice), "Strawberry Fields Forever" (tambourine), "Being For The Benefit Of Mr Kite" (harmonica), "Magical Mystery Tour" (various percussion), "You Know My Name, Look Up The Number" (spade in gravel), "Helter Skelter" (trumpet), "What's The New Mary Jane" (possibly handbell), "Dear Prudence" (backing vocals, handclaps), "Birthday" (handclaps), and "Maxwell's Silver Hammer" (anvil).

The highlight of Evans' career with the Beatles, however, must have been August 27, 1965. The big man never made any qualms about the fact that his idol was the King of Rock 'n' roll, even if his wages were paid by the Beatles. So it must have been the most surreal event of Evans' life to find himself suddenly socialising in the Bel Air mansion of Elvis Presley himself. Evans had worn a suit and tie for the occasion, and was reported to have been totally starstruck after shaking Presley's hand.

During the chaos of the Apple years, Evans was given extended responsibilities, and is credited with discovering The Iveys, later Badfinger. He also enjoyed a brief period as a record producer for Apple Records, before finding that business and finances were stronger than loyalty and friendship. Evans kept a regular diary through the Beatle days, and on January 13th 1969 he wrote:

> Paul [McCartney] is really cutting down on the Apple staff members. I was elevated to office boy and I feel very hurt and sad inside—only big boys don't cry. Why I should feel hurt and reason for writing this is ego . . . I thought I was different from other people in my relationship with The Beatles and being loved by them and treated so nice, I felt like one of the family. Seems I fetch and carry. I find it difficult to live on the £38 I take home each week and would love to be like their other friends who buy fantastic homes and have all the alterations done by them, and are still going to ask for a rise. I always tell myself—look, everybody wants to take from, be satisfied, try to give and you will receive. After all this time I have about £70 to my name, but was content and happy. Loving them as I do,

*nothing is too much trouble, because I want to serve them. Feel
a bit better now—EGO?*

It seems some Beatle associates were more equal than others. One
might speculate that his position as dogsbody lost him the respect
of the employers he saw as friends. As a jack of all trades, he never
seemed to settle on one role.

Evans found himself in such dire financial straits by 1969 that
he was forced to ask Harrison for a raise, and when the Beatles
imploded the following year, Evans found himself adrift and out
of work. He roadied again for Lennon and his Plastic Ono Band,
and spent the next few years alternating between sparse production
work and various solo Beatle projects.

When Lennon separated from Yoko Ono and stumbled drunk-
enly around L.A. for a year and a half, Evans was on hand to serve
his old master. Once Lennon had reunited with Ono however, he
was again surplus to requirements.

In 1976, while still living in LA and separated from his wife and
kids, Evans was working on the memoirs of his Beatle days *Living
The Beatles' Legend*. He became increasingly depressed after his wife
requested a divorce, and was drinking and taking pills. Following
a fracas with his partner at his rented house in an L.A. suburb, the
police were called and informed that Evans had a gun. Apparently
drunk and disoriented from valium, Evans refused to drop his gun
upon request, and 36 years ago on January 5, 1976, he was shot several
times. He died instantly, and later was found to be in possession
of an air rifle.

Like his friend and former employer, shot dead four years later,
Evans was 40 years old. Sadly, none of the former Beatles attended
his funeral service or cremation, although Harrison did see that his
wife receive £5,000. Evans became another victim of life after the
Beatles' success, and like Brian Epstein and John Lennon, had his
life cut tragically short.

Evans was there throughout all of Beatlemania, through the
drugs, the fights, the triumphs, the letdowns, the implosion, even

the fisticuffs. No one, aside from Lennon/McCartney/Harrison/Starr, was as exposed as Evans was to the Beatles' incredible rollercoaster ride. As yet, no book has been published from his memoirs. This unique fly-on-the-wall witnessed it all. Evans, the old workhorse and real unsung hero of the Beatles' incredible saga, could have told some stories.

∾

"The Beatles Roadmanager and Gentle Giant Remembered, 36 Years After His Death," Joe Rodgers. Copyright Dinosaur Album Guides.

[EIGHTEEN]

What Makes Sgt. Pepper So Special?

By Dave Bidini

John, Paul, George, and Ringo tired of the wear-and-tear of
touring. While a great commercial success, the Shea Stadium
performance was for them just another gig where they couldn't
hear themselves play over the hordes of screaming fans. So they
stopped playing live in 1966 and devoted themselves to the studio.
After months of experimentation, the Beatles released the Holy
Grail of Rock music that is Sgt. Pepper's Lonely Hearts Club Band.
But what makes the album so special? —L.M.

∾

R eleased 45 years ago—June 1, 1967—it isn't even the greatest Beatles' record. By comparison, *Rubber Soul* has more full-throttle
joy and rib-sticking melody; *Revolver* is more poignantly genre-bust-
ing; The White Album is more wildly diverse and serious-minded;
Let it Be is bloodier, rawer, more visceral; and *Abbey Road* is more
progressive, and with better George songs. As a concept—based on

an invented band (or bandleader)—the album is a failure. Stretching only so deep as the record's first two songs, the concept is abandoned after the introduction of Billy Shears in favour of a string of unrelated compositions leading to the universal triumph of the album's best (and only great) track, "A Day in the Life." Nothing about what comes before hints at the emotional intensity of the closing number, which leaves Billy Shears in a jumble of bones and carnival serge.

And yet *Sgt. Pepper's Lonely Hearts Club Band* is still the greatest album ever made.

> *In 1967, I was just getting into music. The prehype on Sgt. Pepper was intense. I was living in Windsor, Ont., and convinced my mom I had to take the bus downtown because The Warehouse was opening at midnight to sell the new Beatles album. Against her better wishes, I took the bus downtown so I could be one of the first to buy it. I was surprised there were only six or seven of us there to buy the album, but with money earned cutting grass, I made my purchase. The buses had stopped running, but I took a taxi home, tore off the cellophane, put on my headphones and sat back for the experience of my life. I was profoundly disappointed. Where were the singles? (I was a bubblegum kind of teenager). What was this Within You Without You thing? I remember liking She's Leaving Home. The next day, I traded the album to a friend for 14 45s of my choice. I've since bought Sgt. Pepper a few times and while I'll never consider it my favourite Beatles' album, I now appreciate its brilliance — Kevin Shea, author.*

The album opens with an original and novel device: singing a song that announces the album's concept as well as its name. The track is adorned with fanfare horns and bits of theatre applause and a sidewinding guitar riff that, in an instant, created melodic hard rock: giving the world Cheap Trick and Rick Derringer and Boston and Free before they knew it themselves. The song is short, too, though not small: George Martin juices the kick and snare so that the listener feels as if they're being bounced on a enormous trampoline. But at its apex, the tune ends before giving way to the next track, which, musically, has little to do with the main title. As a concept record, *Sgt. Pepper's* isn't *Tommy* or *SF Sorrow*. It isn't even *Odessa* by the Bee Gees.

Yet it is still the greatest album ever made.

The Beatles were the only rock band my parents ever liked. In their record collection was With the Beatles, the red singles album and Sgt. Pepper. They bought it in London the week it came out; the same week they were married, in a synagogue that, in an odd coincidence, is on Abbey Road. In my house, growing up, it was the sound of happiness. — Geoff Berner, musician.

Paul McCartney's cool Carole Kaye bass line and John Lennon's heavy Scouse backups aside, that "From My Friends" is as well-known for being the track that broke Joe Cocker in America as it is a Beatles' staple proves how low it ranks in terms of the Fab Four's greatest compositions. Musical forensics tell us that the song's vocalist—Ringo—is supposed to be playing Billy Shears in the song, but it's impossible not to associate the Beatles' singers with being anyone but themselves. Here, the Most Fortunate Musician in the History of Rock 'n' Roll does a swell job rising from his drum stool to stand at his star point, but, after two songs, there's nothing we haven't heard before.

And yet.

When I was six years old, my aunt put a giant pair of head-phones on me and said, "Come and get me when Side 1 is over." I wasn't sure if I'd be able to handle the whole album let alone one side, but it was life-changing. For a kid used to disco and the Top 40, it was a real trip. — Bob Campbell, tehnician.

Left to John Lennon, *Sgt. Pepper* finally does something. But if "Lucy in the Sky with Diamonds" gazes deep at a new horizon of sound with its sand mosaic of glinting keyboards and crying smile vocals—recorded, famously, through a whirring Leslie cabinet—it also establishes two different musical agendas: Paul's buoyant pop and John's introspective psychedelia. As a result, *Sgt. Pepper's* lacks the natural cohesion of *Revolver* because the gulf between these musical differences is broader. In the context of the album, "Lucy" is another jigsaw square that doesn't quite fit, and the chorus, in its own way, still sounds as heavy as anything in rock 'n' roll; affording the lyrics weight beyond that of an acid-soaked couch creature would be to bejewel a baby too young and dopey to know the real world.

The album's next track, "Getting Better," is, arguably, McCartney's finest moment here, but fine only so far as it's evocative of something on *Revolver*: pop music that makes you feel as if you're walking alone in a city crowd while rising about two feet above everyone else for reasons you can't quite establish. In other words, deep and worthy of veneration. "Getting Better" is not, and neither is the next McCartney track (of three consecutive), "Fixing a Hole," which overstays its establishing melody and lyrical swerve that taps into Lennonesque trippiness ("I'm painting my room in the colourful way") from the relatively sober perspective of a pintsman. Paul's musical triptych is rescued, in part, by "She's Leaving Home," which some have described as taking the lyrical form of a short story. This may be true, but the characters aren't half as affecting as those in "Eleanor Rigby." Heard beyond a forgiving mood, "She's Leaving Home" sounds lachrymose. It also starts with a harp. Where you stand on that instrument affects your position concerning the quality of the song.

And yet.

I was born the year Sgt. Pepper's was released. When I turned eight, I vividly recall playing the album in my older sister's bedroom on her turntable when she wasn't there, and weeping at the lyrics of She's Leaving Home. My eldest sister, who was 14 years my senior, had a falling out with my parents and left when I was seven. She was 21. For a lot of years, she was in the

*world somewhere, but not in touch with us. I knew I had this
older sister and I used to think about her lots and wondered
where she was, what she was doing, who she was, etc. It was my
second older sister who was crazy about the Beatles and whose
vinyl I played that morning. I played that song over and over
and, like the characters in the song, I wished she'd come home
so I could get to know her. She eventually got back in touch
with the family. I still feel as if I don't know her well. — Jill
Castle, designer.*

"Being for the Benefit of Mr. Kite!" is a wild composition—as adult
as "Getting Better" is teenage—with nightmarish keyboards and
grotesque lyrics; the aural equivalent of a book by Edward Gorey.
But for fans of "In My Life" or "Help!" or "She Said, She Said" or
"Nowhere Man" —Lennon's finest pre-*Pepper* songs— "Mr. Kite"
provides no keyhole into the heart of the composer. Instead, it's just
another Clue character number, like "Lovely Rita" or "Sexy Sadie."
Perhaps its resonance was the result of something that sounded like
whatever everyone else was thinking: melodic acid, hallucinatory
rhymes, and stoner drumming. Coming only two months before
The Piper at the Gates of Dawn, timing is often everything.

Yet *Sgt. Pepper's Lonely Hearts Club Band* is still the greatest
album ever made.

*Sgt. Pepper's was released the day I was born. The first time I
heard it all the way through, I was about seven, and I couldn't
stop staring at the photo on the gatefold. They seemed best of
chums. In retrospect, McCartney was already starting to bug
everyone else and they were all totally baked in the photo. But
at the time, they were chums, and gods. I loved that Macca
had the OPP badge on his arm because my brother had just
become a cop. It was a purple vinyl edition (or maybe yellow),
but it seemed like a cohesive "concept" record that worked when
I heard it then. I was mesmerized, and I've spent the last 38*

years trying to earn my way into the band. —Dave Merritt, Golden Seals.

"Within You Without You."
No.

Following George's raga, the second half of the album continues with "When I'm Sixty-Four," which as many Beatles fans love as others despise. There's something innately charming about the antique nature of the song, and something profound and even brave about including a Hoagy Carmichael-style ditty on a record that was, in its time, cutting-edge. But if the Beatles were world-beating innovators who did what no other band dared to do, "When I'm Sixty-Four" grooved no new path. Instead, it laid in the loam, imagining a time before cars and drugs and rock 'n' roll and dreaming of old age, pain medication and retirement.

And yet.

Even though they were created by the greatest musical ensemble ever at the ostensible height of their powers, both "Lovely Rita" and "Good Morning Good Morning" are filler, and great albums aren't supposed to have filler. Neither will ever be packaged on a greatest hits collection or studied by young artists hoping to understand how great songs are made. And yet, in spite of these tracks—and a few others like them—*Sgt. Pepper's Lonely Hearts Club Band* is still the greatest album ever made.

This leaves us with one question: why?

We were living in North York, the suburbs of Toronto. I was seven years old. My older brother Peter was actually the one who got the album first. Even by this young age, I was already indoctrinated into what would be a lifelong cult, a clinical Beatlemaniac before my 10th birthday. Seeing the elaborate Peter Blake album art for the first time was my own non-pharmaceutical version of an acid trip. Was this the same Fab Four I'd had innocent boy crushes on? If the album art was a trip, the music was positively surreal. I was a singles, AM radio kid, and wasn't "into" deep album cuts like "Tomorrow Never Knows" from Revolver, at the time, so I hadn't seen the psychedelic writing on the wall. But for some reason—perhaps the media scrutiny surrounding Pepper—my brothers and I decided to go through this album, track by track, in sequence. I didn't know big words like "eclectic" at the time, but the variety of styles on hand, from cut to cut, felt like the rules were being rewritten around me. If this was a pop album, I had better get to know the new rules, even if they seemed doomed to be broken by the next track. The fear of Pepper's turned into delight. — Paul Myers, musician/author.

Because no other record possesses a song as great as "A Day in the Life," *Sgt. Pepper's Lonely Hearts Club Band* is still the greatest album ever made. The track feels and sounds and plays as epic as life itself; one part as good as the next; layered with textures and images both poetic and real; and performed both quietly and powerfully before ending with a single chord that echoes the very pulse of humanity, which, in 1967, put colours and sound to a civilization bursting with life. "A Day in the Life" is where understanding and uncertainty meet; you think you know it, but you don't know it at all, even after 45 years. It is pop and neoclassical; rock and music hall; prog and folk; hard and soft; Paul and John; sad and beautiful; and every feeling in between. Had it not brought down the curtain on the Billy Shears' show—coming after a quick Pepper reprise; a commercial trailer for the album—I would not be writing this story and the world of art and music would be very different. Not worse or better. Just different.

And that's why.

[NINETEEN]

The Real "Lucy in the Sky with Diamonds"

By Associated Press Staff

In case you still thought John was trying to abscond the truth about "Lucy in the Sky with Diamonds" being about LSD, here's the living (or deceased proof) that his story for the inspiration of the revered song holds up. —L.M.

Lucy Vodden, who provided the inspiration for the Beatles' classic song "Lucy in the Sky With Diamonds," has died after a long battle with lupus. She was 46.

Her death was announced Monday by St. Thomas' Hospital in London, where she had been treated for the chronic disease for more than five years, and by her husband, Ross Vodden. Britain's Press Association said she died last Tuesday. Hospital officials said they could not confirm the day of her death.

Mrs. Vodden's connection to the Beatles dates back to her early days, when she made friends with schoolmate Julian Lennon, John

Lennon's son. Julian Lennon, then 4 years old, came home from school with a drawing one day, showed it to his father and said it was "Lucy in the sky with diamonds."

At the time, John Lennon was gathering material for his contributions to *Sgt. Pepper's Lonely Hearts Club Band*, a landmark album released to worldwide acclaim in 1967.

The elder Lennon seized on the image and developed it into what is widely regarded as a psychedelic masterpiece, replete with haunting images of "newspaper taxis" and a "girl with kaleidoscope eyes."

Rock music critics thought the song's title was a veiled reference to LSD, but John Lennon always claimed the phrase came from his son, not from a desire to spell out the initials LSD in code.

Mrs. Vodden lost touch with Julian Lennon after he left the school following his parents' divorce, but they were reunited in recent years when Julian Lennon, who lives in France, tried to help her cope with the disease.

He sent her flowers and vouchers for use at a gardening center near her home in Surrey in southeast England, and frequently sent her text messages in an effort to buttress her spirits.

"I wasn't sure at first how to approach her," Julian Lennon told the Associated Press in June. "I wanted at least to get a note to her. Then I heard she had a great love of gardening, and I thought I'd help with something she's passionate about, and I love gardening too. I wanted to do something to put a smile on her face."

In recent months, Mrs. Vodden was too ill to go out most of the time, except for hospital visits.

She enjoyed her link to the Beatles but was not particularly fond of "Lucy in the Sky With Diamonds."

"I don't relate to the song, to that type of song," she told the Associated Press in June. "As a teenager, I made the mistake of telling a couple of friends at school that I was the Lucy in the song and they said, 'No, it's not you, my parents said it's about drugs.' And I didn't know what LSD was at the time, so I just kept it quiet, to myself."

Mrs. Vodden is the latest in a long line of people connected to the Beatles who died at a relatively young age.

The list includes John Lennon, gunned down at age 40; manager Brian Epstein, who died of a drug overdose when he was 32; and original band member Stuart Sutcliffe, who died of a brain hemorrhage at 21.

A spokeswoman for Julian Lennon and his mother, Cynthia Lennon, said they were "shocked and saddened" by Mrs. Vodden's death.

Angie Davidson, a lupus sufferer who is campaign director of the St. Thomas' Lupus Trust, said Mrs. Vodden was "a real fighter" who had worked behind the scenes to support efforts to combat the disease.

"It's so sad that she has finally lost the battle she fought so bravely for so long," Ms. Davidson said.

∾

[TWENTY]

Religion and the Beatles

By Washington Times Staff

The Beatles were like any one of us—ordinary people trying to find meaning in their lives. Each went through his own spiritual journey. And the end of the hectic touring schedules in the latter part of 1966 afforded them more time for spiritual exploration that took the form of drug use, reading, and a prolonged stay at the compound of Maharishi Mahesh Yogi. The influence of this is apparent in the more mature, insightful lyrical content of their later music. —L.M.

They met at a church party. John was an Anglican choirboy, and Paul was a not-very-active Catholic. And the band they created, John would later claim, became "more popular than Jesus."

The Fab Four made it commonplace to mix rock 'n' roll and religion, says Steve Turner, author of *The Gospel According to the Beatles*.

"You could have 'The Gospel According to Karl Marx," Mr.

Turner says. "Anyone who has thought there is something not quite right with the world and reckoned they've got a solution to offer, however profound or not so profound the solution might be, you could say that is a gospel."

His book details the religious background and personal beliefs of John Lennon, Paul McCartney, George Harrison and Ringo Starr and examines how spirituality manifested itself in their music. Freeing people's minds and expanding their consciousness are at the heart of the Beatles' gospel, along with love, peace, hope, truth, honesty and transcendence, Mr. Turner says.

"They talk about the problem that we are somehow blind or misunderstanding things," Mr. Turner says. "You needed to open up your mind, so everything you experienced had much more impact on you."

Like other pop culture sensations, the Beatles communicated cultural values and provided a social critique, says William D. Romanowski, author of *Eyes Wide Open: Looking for God in Popular Culture*.

"The Beatles were a unique and unprecedented phenomenon in popular music," says Mr. Romanowski, professor of communication arts and sciences at Calvin College in Grand Rapids, Mich. "They took rock 'n' roll to a new level in musical sophistication and thematic content."

Although Eastern religions such as Hinduism and Zen Buddhism later influenced the Beatles' outlook, Mr. Lennon and Mr. Starr had been baptized as Anglicans, and Mr. McCartney and Mr. Harrison as Roman Catholics.

However, Mr. Lennon was the only one raised in church. He knew a fair amount of Christian theology from the Church of England Sunday school lessons and Bible classes, Mr. Turner says. On July 6, 1957, Mr. Lennon first met Mr. McCartney in the halls of St. Peter's Church in the Liverpool neighborhood of Woolton, when Mr. Lennon's first band, the Quarrymen, played at the church's annual garden party.

Abandoned by his father, Mr. Lennon was raised largely by aunt

Mimi Smith. She was a strict disciplinarian who made sure young John attended church. From the time Mr. Lennon was a teenager, he drew blasphemous pictures, and Jesus became a figure against whom Mr. Lennon compared himself and reconsidered throughout his life, Mr. Turner says.

"Christianity wasn't such a big influence in [Mr. McCartney's] background," Mr. Turner says. "It's got to loom pretty large in your background for you to want to mock it."

The differences in Mr. Lennon's and Mr. McCartney's experience of faith informed their songwriting, Mr. Turner says, noting that Mr. Lennon's song "Imagine" supposes that "there is no heaven," but songs such as "Let it Be," "Lady Madonna" and "Eleanor Rigby"—chiefly composed by Mr. McCartney—use Catholic imagery.

In 1967, when the Beatles met with Maharishi Mahesh Yogi, the resulting publicity introduced many people in the West to Transcendental Meditation, Mr. Turner says. Mr. McCartney later said, "If we had met the Maharishi before we had taken LSD, we wouldn't have needed to take it."

When Mr. Turner interviewed Mr. Lennon in 1971, Mr. Lennon said he didn't believe in God. However, in 1972, Mr. Lennon corresponded with evangelist Oral Roberts, inquiring about Christianity. In spring 1977, Mr. Lennon told friends that he had become a born-again Christian. His profession of faith lasted about eight weeks, mostly because of Yoko Ono, his wife, Mr. Turner says.

Mr. Lennon changed his views often. At one point, he showed interest in trepanation, a belief that drilling a hole in the skull can expand consciousness. In final interviews before he was fatally shot in 1980, Mr. Lennon talked about wanting to re-examine New Testament parables.

"If it was a machine or a technique or whatever, John would have a try," Mr. Turner says. "He would sometimes talk about being aware of a greater power or energy. He might have called it 'God' at some point. I don't think he was ever not an atheist, except for the brief time in the '70s.

Other members of the Beatles continued to experience spirituality in different ways, Mr. Turner says, with Mr. McCartney making causes such as vegetarianism and environmentalism his religion. Mr. Harrison was associated with the Hare Krishna movement until his death in 2001. On Mr. Starr's 2005 album, *Choose Love*, the song "Oh My Lord" asks for help when he is "dark and full of fear." In recent years, Mr. Starr reportedly has attended Alcoholic Anonymous meetings, where "a higher power" is endorsed.

"The Beatles raised a lot of good questions," Mr. Turner says. "I personally found it quite encouraging at the time, because I always thought religion seemed to be on a divergent path to rock 'n' roll."

The Beatles should be credited for ushering in the "Jesus Music" of the 1960s and 1970s—pioneered by performers such as Larry Norman—which was the Christian component of the hippie counterculture, says Mark Joseph, author of "Faith, God, & Rock 'n' Roll."

"Until then, rock was hesitant to get into spirituality and religion," says Mr. Joseph, producer of "The Passion of the Christ" CD.

Years after Mr. Lennon penned his song "God," which says, "I don't believe in Jesus," U2 responded with "God Part II," Mr. Joseph said. U2 songs such as "God Part II" and "Grace" contrast the idea of "karma" espoused by the Eastern religions explored by the Beatles, Mr. Joseph says.

U2 lead singer Bono has spoken of the "mind-blowing concept that the God who created the universe might be looking for company, a real relationship with people," and told author Michka Assayas, "The thing that keeps me on my knees is the difference between grace and karma."

Although many churches in the 1960s protested the Beatles, today's churches are more attuned to popular culture, Mr. Joseph says.

"The church refused to engage the Beatles, so Bono took it up 20 years later," he says. "Instead of saying, 'Those guys are hippies, doing drugs,' the songs deserved to be engaged. You can agree or disagree, but you should engage them."

∽

[TWENTY-ONE]

Before Yoko: A Girl Named Cyn

By Chris Maume

The great irony of John Lennon's life was that the trauma perpetually haunting him was his parents' abandonment—and yet he abandoned his own wife and son. John had a love-hate relationship with Cynthia Powell from the beginning, sometimes professing his love for her, then suddenly treating her cruelly. Tragically, John married Cynthia at a time when he didn't really know what he wanted out of life. When he seemingly found what he wanted, it was to the misfortune of the woman who had been there with devotion from the beginning. —L.M.

⁓

Cynthia Lennon knew her days as a Beatle wife were over when she walked into the house in Weybridge she shared with John Lennon after a holiday in Greece to find her husband in a bathrobe sitting on the floor with Yoko Ono. The guest room showed no signs of having been slept in; she turned around and walked out of the door. They had spent the night recording their experimental *Two Virgins* album and had then made love.

There was a brief reconciliation, but when Cynthia went away for a short break to Italy, Ono moved in and Cynthia and John were soon divorced. It was the end of a relationship in which, almost from the beginning, she was used by Lennon, getting almost nothing in return. Though he become the spokesman for the peace-and-love generation, he treated Cynthia and their son, Julian, cruelly.

Cynthia Powell was born in 1939 in a boarding house in Blackpool, to where her mother had been evacuated. Her parents were Liverpudlians; her father Charles was a travelling electrical goods salesman who died of lung cancer in 1956; he and Cynthia's mother, Lillian, lived in Hoylake on the Wirral. It was genteel compared to the city across the Mersey; when she and John met at Liverpool College of Art, she was the butt of his jokes: "Quiet, please," he would shout. "No dirty jokes, it's Cynthia."

They took one class together, Lettering, and one day, quite unexpectedly, when she saw another girl stroke his neck she felt a pang of jealousy. Eventually, at a party in July 1959, they danced a slow dance. As she recalls in her memoir, *A Twist of Lennon*, John asked her out, and when she said she was engaged to a chap in Hoylake—in fact she had been, to a window-cleaner called Barry, but it was over—he replied, "I didn't ask you to marry me, did I?"

As she was leaving the party she heard Lennon's voice: "Don't you know Cynthia's a nun?" Goaded, she went back into the party; later that night she and Lennon went to bed.

The relationship was rocky from the start. Like every parent he'd ever met, the domineering Lillian couldn't bear Lennon. And she had a point.

Cynthia recalled his violent possessiveness and "unreasonable rages . . . I was really quite terrified of him for 75 per cent of the time." But the bond grew stronger, despite John's serial infidelities, and when he went off to Hamburg with the Beatles she moved in with his guardian, Aunt Mimi.

Then, in April 1962, she found she was pregnant, and they married at Mount Pleasant registry office in Liverpool. The Beatles were on the brink of global stardom, and on the insistence of their new manager, Brian Epstein, the pregnancy and marriage were to remain secret for as long as possible.

Julian was born in April 1963, by which time Beatlemania was getting into its stride. After living at John's Aunt Mimi's for a while they moved to London, where their flat was permanently besieged by screaming fans (she was attacked by one fan as late as 1967).

Life in the Beatles vortex was never comfortable: the couple moved into their posh house in Surrey, where Cynthia raised Julian mostly on her own (Lennon's callous treatment of his son famously inspired Paul McCartney to write "Hey Jude"). Lennon began to consume huge amounts of LSD, which she said was the beginning of the end for their relationship. She was slipped the drug by John's dentist at a dinner party, and recalled, "It was if we suddenly found ourselves in the middle of a horror film."

Innately conservative, she was left behind by the rock'n'roll lifestyle, and it was symbolic that when the band caught the train to Bangor in 1967 to meet the Maharishi Mahesh Yogi she was left on the platform. She did travel with the band to the Maharishi's ashram in India, though the experience prompted John, on the flight home, to confess to all his infidelities. It was a long list.

At first John sued for divorce on the grounds of Cynthia's supposed adultery with a hotelier, Roberto Bassanini, who she had met during her short break to Italy, but when Yoko became pregnant (later miscarrying) Cynthia countersued. She agreed to a settlement of £100,000, with a further £100,000 put in trust for Julian.

She married Bassanini in 1970, divorcing him in 1973. A third marriage, to John Twist, an engineer from Lancashire, followed; after they parted in 1983 she changed her name back to "Lennon" by deed poll and met Jim Christie, her partner for 17 years. She published a memoir, A Twist of Lennon, in 1978, but in 1991 she auctioned off all her John-related memorabilia. In 2002 she married Noel Charles, a Bajan nightclub owner; he died in 2013.

For a time she had a restaurant, Lennon's, in the West End; she kept her artistic hand in all the while, and had several exhibitions of her paintings, while in 1984 she made the ceramics that adorn the doorways in Cavern Walks. In 2005, she published a more intimate biography, John. Although she made continual attempts to move on with her life, it was a life almost inevitably dominated by her relationship with one of the most famous men in the world. She died after a short bout of cancer.

∼

[TWENTY-TWO]

George Harrison, Pattie Boyd and Eric Clapton

By Bill Harry

John wasn't the only one who had trouble with women. In fact, all four of the Beatles had a history infidelity in their younger years. But George's relationship with Pattie Boyd stands out for being mutually-destructive. —L.M.

George's first wife, Pattie was born Patricia Anne Boyd in Hampstead, London, on 17 March 1944, the eldest of three sisters. Due to their father's job the family moved to Kenya in the 1950s and didn't return until Pattie was in her late teens.

Pattie and her sister Jenny first arrived in London in 1962 with ambitions of becoming models. Pattie was initially brought to the attention of the British public when she appeared in a series of television commercials for Smith's Crisps. Dick Lester produced the commercials and when he was commissioned to direct the Beatles' debut movie *A Hard Day's Night*, he booked Pattie for the role of one of the schoolgirls who meet the Beatles on a train traveling from Liverpool to London.

Her part was cut down to one line and when the Beatles describe how they feel like prisoners, she had one word of dialogue "Prisoners?"

She arrived on the first day of filming and was to say, "I met them and they said hello. I couldn't believe it. They were so like how I'd imagined them to be. They were just like pictures of themselves coming to life. George hardly said hello. But the others came and chatted with us."

When filming began Pattie said she could feel George looking at her and was embarrassed. She was also terrified of John and when she came to ask for their autographs near the end of the first day's shooting, she was too scared to ask for John's. John was later to refer to her as Batty Pattie. When she asked George for his autograph she asked him if he could sign for her two sisters, Jenny and Paula, as well. He put two kisses under the autographs for the two sisters and seven kisses under the autograph for Pattie.

He came into the carriage where Pattie was sitting with another girl, Pru and asked her to come out into the corridor on her own. He asked if she would go out with him that night and she said no. This was because she had a steady boyfriend, 30 year old photographer Eric Swayne, who she'd been going out with for two years. The following Tuesday George asked her out again. This time she told her boyfriend it was all over and accepted George's invitation.

She recalled, "Eric was my boyfriend, but not any more. George is tremendous fun to be with. We want it to stay just fun without having to talk about engagements and marriages."

George was enchanted by her and said she reminded him of his favourite film star, Brigitte Bardot. By the end of the week she'd introduced him to her mother and sisters. He said, "She's my kind of girl and we like each other a lot, but marriage is not on our minds. We hope to see more of each other when we can. It isn't a sin to have a girlfriend is it?"

The following week was Easter and Pattie and George joined

John and Cynthia for a weekend in Ireland at Dromoland Castle Hotel, but they were hounded by the press.

George, who, more than any of the other members of the Beatles, treasured his privacy, was furious when the hotel was besieged by reporters who covered every doorway and exit, asking. "Who's the blonde, George?" and "What's her name?" and "Do you love her?" The couples were left stranded in their rooms, with George saying. "Don't we give those bastards a big enough pound of flesh every goddamn day of our lives? Why can't they just leave us alone sometimes?"

Pattie and Cynthia had to dress up as maids and were smuggled out of the rear entrance in a laundry basket and driven to the airport in a laundry van. Then they went to Waikiki in Hawaii between 5 May and 20 May 1964. When they stopped over in Los Angeles they were spotted by photographers and George told them that Pattie was "my 29-year-old sister. My chaperone."

By the end of the month George took her to see a bungalow he was considering buying in Esher. The bungalow was called Kinfauns and within four weeks George had bought it for the two of them to live in together. He proposed to her on Christmas Day 1963.

Pattie was to say, "We lived together for about a year before we got married. My mother knew, but she never mentioned it."

She then began to receive nasty letters from fans and was unprepared for the hostility, which she found frightening. She recalled, "Hordes of wretched little girls used to lie in wait outside our gate waiting for me to go out to the shops. I was regularly kicked, bitten and even punched solely because I was George's girlfriend. "You'd better leave off our George or else", they would shout as I drove away. George attempted to talk to them about it, but every time he came round they just fell about swooning and giggling. The next morning, however, once again they'd be out in full force, screaming insults and sometimes actually threatening to murder me."

The press interest, the crowds and the threatening letters worried Pattie, also the physical attacks by female fans, which were the lot of Beatles wives and girlfriends.

Once, when she went to The Beatles Christmas Show in Hammersmith with Terry Doran, a group of girls started punching her. Then they took their shoes off and shouted, "Let's get her." They started kicking her and Pattie punched one in the face while Terry got one against the wall and held her tight. They were shouting and swearing, but Pattie managed to escape. However, she was to become a popular figure with teenagers and wrote a column on the British rock scene for America's 16 Magazine called 'Pattie's Letter From London'.

For a time she set up a clothes stall with her sisters called 'Juniper', named after the song Donovan wrote about her sister, 'Jennifer Juniper.'

George actually had to ask Brian Epstein for permission to get married. He drove to Brian's house in Chapel Street, Belgravia in December 1965 and left Pattie in the car outside while he went in to see his manager. He emerged ten minutes later to tell Pattie: "It's all right. Brian has said we can get married in January. Off we go!" Pattie commented, "God has spoken!"

When John Lennon was told, he said, "January's a bit soon, she must be in the club."

Commenting on the romance, George's father Harry said, "When George got together with Pattie, Mrs. Harrison and I were delighted. Of course, to the rest of the world it might have been 'Beatle marries model', but to those that really knew them it was clear that this was a genuine modern-day love story."

The couple were wed at Epsom Register Office, Surrey on Friday 21 January 1966, with Paul McCartney in attendance, and spent their honeymoon in Barbados. When George was busy touring it was Pattie who became interested in spiritual matters. Pattie revealed that her interest in religion had been sparked by the trip she and George made to India in September 1966, although the trip had been made simply for George to study Indian music.

Of the five weeks spent in India, she commented, "We had really gone so George could study the sitar under Ravi Shankar. We met Ravi's guru, his spiritual guide. You can't be in India without being aware of everything. We went to a meeting at Benares, the Holy City on the Ganges. Millions of people had come for a big festival which went on for three days."

On their return she had lots of time on her hands. George, with his obsession for privacy and keeping the media at arms length, had told Pattie she had to give up all her modeling work. When she became interested in charity work, he forbade her doing that, too. Her thoughts turned to an interest in the spirituality she detected during her trip to India and she went along to Caxton Hall in London in February 1967 to listen to a lecture by the Maharishi Mahesh Yogi on his Spiritual Regeneration Movement.

So Pattie became the first member of the Beatles' circle to join the Maharishi Mahesh Yogi's Spiritual Regeneration movement, and she was so impressed she talked George and the other members of the Beatles into attending his lecture on Transcendental Meditation at the Hilton Hotel in Park Lane, London on Thursday 24 August 1967. Those of their party in attendance were George and Pattie, John and Cynthia and Paul and Jane Asher. Following his lecture, the Maharishi gave them a private audience. As a result of this meeting, they all began a ten-day course on Transcendental Meditation, held at University College, Bangor, in North Wales.

The seminar was marred by the tragic news that Brian Epstein, who had intended to join them at the seminar, had been found dead.

Her vivacity and beauty made headlines. She was an ideal Beatles bride in the eyes of the media, and proved to be the inspiration for several of George's songs, including 'Something', 'If I Needed Someone', 'For You Blue' and 'It's All Too Much'. After six years of marriage, however, the couple began to drift apart.

Since George had frowned on her having a modeling career, the 26-year-old Pattie felt isolated in the large Friar Park mansion they had moved into in 1970. She wanted to raise a family but never seemed to get pregnant and both of them went for fertility tests. Pattie was willing to adopt a child, but George wasn't. Gradually, they began to engage in arguments. Against George's wishes she decided to become a model again and agreed to appear in an Ozzie

Clark fashion show. Then, during a dinner with Ringo and his wife Maureen, George declared that he was in love with Maureen.

A tearful Pattie fled to the bathroom and his guests left. It was alleged that a few weeks later, when Pattie returned from a shopping trip, she found George and Maureen in bed together.

When someone asked him, "How could you, with your best friend's wife?"

An unperturbed George said, "Incest, I guess."

Towards the end of 1973, Pattie had her first extramarital affair, with Ronnie Wood, who was then a member of the Faces. Or rather, she took part in a wife-swapping episode, which was ideal fare for the tabloids.

In October 1973 Ronnie and his wife Chrissie had been invited to stay at Friar Park for a month as George's guests. During the month, Wood reportedly had a liaison with Pattie and on Monday 26 November 1973 he issued a statement; "My romance with Pattie Boyd is definitely on. Things will be sorted out in a few days. Until then, I naturally can't say very much. We're going to talk it out between us and hope to get a happy arrangement. Meanwhile, Pattie has gone back to her home and will be talking to George about it. I won't be seeing her today."

When George read the statement, he said, "Whatever Ronnie Wood has got to say about anything, certainly about us, it has nothing to do with Pattie or me. Got that! It has nothing to do with us, her or me!"

Some years later Chrissie exposed the relationship in *The News of the World* and reported that she and George had gone on holiday in Portugal and Switzerland while Pattie and Wood were holidaying in the Bahamas.

In 1974 news also came out about an affair between George and the actress Kathy Simmonds. Kathy, who'd had affairs with Rod Stewart and Harry Nilsson, spent several weeks with George in a villa at St. George's Bay in Grenada. Kathy believed that the romance was serious. Then George suddenly left her, flying to Los Angeles to discuss his forthcoming American tour.

The most visible episode of the drifting relationship was the interest Eric Clapton took in George's wife.

Eric had been a friend of George from when they first met in 1964 when he was a member of the Yardbirds. Eric first met Pattie in 1969 at Cream's Farewell Concert (although some say it was at a party at Brian Epstein's house). He recalled, "I fell in love with her at first sight and it got heavier and heavier for me. I remember feeling a dreadful emptiness because I was certain I was never going to meet a woman quite that beautiful for myself."

In 1969 Clapton bought a house near the Harrison's and became a frequent visitor to their mansion Friar Park in Henley-on-Thames.

He was later to say, "What I couldn't accept was that she was out of reach for me. She was married to George and he was a mate but I had fallen in love and nobody else mattered."

He was so obsessed he began an affair with her sister Paula, who looked a lot like Pattie and had the same kind of personality.

Pattie was not unaware of the interest Eric showed in her. In an effort to revive George's interest, or to make him jealous, she began to flirt with Eric.

Eric wrote a song declaring his love, which he based on a 1,000-year-old Persian book by Nizami called 'Layla and Majnun'. The song 'Layla' was included on an album Eric made under the pseudonym Derek & the Dominoes and George was invited to play on it. The number entered the British Top 10 in 1972 and again in 1982.

Eric phoned her one day in 1970 and expressed his love. Pattie told him she loved George. "I couldn't believe the situation Eric had put me in. I thought it wasn't right and I thought that our friendship was destined to end."

Eric sent an unsigned letter saying he needed to see her, that he loved her. She took it to George, who assumed it was from a crazy person. Eric called her and confessed about the letter.

George was busy working on *All Things Must Pass*. The couple were due to see the controversial play 'Oh Calcutta.' Patti went alone (some reports said she went with Eric, others that he met her there). He asked her to come to his house to listen to the Derek and the

Dominoes recording and played her 'Layla.' They made love. At the after-show party, George arrived and spotted Eric and Pattie hand in hand. He shouted at Eric that he was never to see Pattie again and shoved her into the car.

The couple began to grow more and more apart and Eric still desired Pattie.

George was to comment, "Actually, Pattie and I had been splitting up for years. That was the funny thing, you know. I thought that was the best thing to do, for us to split and we should have done it much sooner. But I didn't have any problem about it. Eric had the problem. Every time I'd go and see him, he'd be really hung up about it, and I was saying, 'Fuck it, man, don't be apologizing,' and he didn't believe me. I was saying, 'I don't care!'"

Pattie said, "I felt terrible guilt. Eric kept insisting I should leave George and go and live with him. I said I couldn't. I got cold feet. I couldn't bear it."

Eric said, "I told her that either she came with me or I hit the deck. I actually presented her with a packet of heroin and said, 'If you don't come with me, I'm taking this for the next couple of years.' I put dreadful pressure on her, but I couldn't help myself. I really could not visualize a life without her. Well, the pressure from me must have been so great that she went back and closed herself back into the house with George."

On 14 February 1972 George and Pattie were involved in a car accident on the M4 motorway near Maidenhead, on their way back from Friar Park and they were taken to Maidenhead Hospital. Pattie suffered the most serious injuries with concussion and several broken ribs

In 1974 George went on a trip to India without Pattie. She flew to Los Angeles to spend some time with her sister Jenny, who was married to Mick Fleetwood of Fleetwood Mac. Then she flew to Miami to join Eric who was recording his album '461 Ocean Boulevard' there. She claimed she did that because she thought she would manipulate Eric in order to recapture George. She then felt she'd fallen in love with Eric.

When George arrived back in London Pattie told him she was going with Eric again and wouldn't be coming back.

He said, "It's no big deal. We've separated many times but this time I don't know what will happen. In this life, there is no time to lose in an uncomfortable situation."

George was also quoted as saying, "If she had to go off with someone, better Eric than some dope."

At a party on the completion of '461 Ocean Boulevard', Eric recalled, "I went straight up to him and said, 'I'm in love with your wife. What are you going to do about it?' George said, 'Whatever you like, man. It doesn't worry me.' He was being very spiritual about it and saying everybody should do their own thing. He then said, 'You can have her and I'll have your girlfriend.'

"I couldn't believe this. I thought he was going to chin me. Pattie freaked out and ran away. Suddenly she was in limbo. George must have been very upset too. But that's crazy! If he didn't want her to leave him, he shouldn't have let me take her."

Eric recalls, 'George, Pattie and I were sitting in the hallway of my house. I remember George saying, 'Well, I suppose I'd better divorce her.' He managed to laugh it all off when I thought it was getting pretty hairy. I thought the whole situation was tense; he thought it was funny. Then he helped us all through the split up."

George invited Eric and Pattie to Friar Park one evening. Another guest present was actor John Hurt. George had laid out two guitars and two small amplifiers and when Eric turned up late with Pattie, George invited him to play; it was the equivalent of a duel, with the woman they loved there to watch. With six people present, the two guitarists played for two hours and spectators say that George had provided Eric with the inferior guitar and amplifier, but the opinion was that Eric won, even though he'd had too many brandies. Eric was to comment, "I know exactly how to play in a situation like that. If someone makes the mistake of exaggerating, or being a bit too flamboyant, you win by being simple. Let them overdo it."

George was to say, "Well, Eric didn't really run off with her because we had kind of finished with each other anyway. And, you know, for me this is what I think is the main problem. I think the fact is that I didn't get annoyed with him and I think that has always annoyed him. I think that deep down inside he wishes that it really pissed me off, but it didn't because I was happy that she went off, because we'd finished together and it made things easier for me, you see, because otherwise we'd have had to go through all those big rows and divorces."

Pattie was divorced from George in 1977 and married Eric on 27 March 1979 at the Apostolic Assembly of Faith in Christ Church, Tucson, Arizona. George and his second wife Olivia Arias were top of the guest list for the wedding, but they didn't attend.

On their return a belated wedding reception was held on 19 May in the back garden of Clapton's home, Hurtwood Edge, in the village of Ewhurst, Surrey, 25 miles from London. George and Olivia were among the 200 celebrity guests. Clapton had hired workmen to erect a platform for a jam session and at 9 p.m. Jim Capaldi sat down on drums. Paul McCartney started playing bass. As the jam went on it featured Ginger Baker on drums, Paul on bass, Denny Laine and eventually Clapton on guitars, George and Ray Cooper (of Elton John fame) on keyboards. Then Paul asked Lonnie Donegan up and Lonnie did a skiffle session. Next it was Paul on bass with Ringo on drums and George, Clapton and Denny on guitars. Then Mick Jagger jumped up and joined them singing the old Eddie Cochran song 'Something Else'.

Problems began once Eric and Pattie settled in at the mansion in Hurtwood Edge. When Eric began to drink to excess, the strain was apparent. She recalled, "It was becoming very difficult. You'd look for the part of the person you knew and loved, but it was hard to find."

Eric and Pattie separated in November 1984. They were back again the following year and she joined him on his American tour. Eric said that the trouble started when he gave up drinking. "I was very dogmatic. I was very strict, in a way that made it difficult for people to relate to me. You see, Pattie likes to drink and I became very strict about that. I started to put her down and I was intolerant. Then I wouldn't take her on tour with me and we drifted apart."

By 1985 Pattie had been publicly humiliated by a number of public affairs Eric had engaged in and the fact that he'd had two children by different women, one a son, Conor, by Lori del Santo. This was particularly hurtful as Pattie was unable to have children.

After they separated she said, "It probably took me six years to get over it, with four years of psychotherapy. My self-esteem was unbelievably low, and I found it really hard to build up relationships because I had been used to difficult people. Anybody who was sweet and nice was no challenge."

Pattie and Eric were married for seven years but they broke up in 1986. Clapton was to say, "We tried and tried to have a child…to the point where it became a pressure, an immense stumbling block to our marriage."

Pattie filed for divorce on 29 April 1988, citing Clapton's adultery with Italian TV personality Lori del Santo, who'd given birth to Clapton's son in August 1987.

She later took up a profession as a photographer working from a studio in the Fulham area of London, where she also settled. In the early 1990s she invested in a modeling agency for older women called Déjà Vu, but it was a financial disappointment. In 1991 she then went on to found a new charity with Ringo Starr's wife Barbara Bach called SHARP (Self Help Addiction Recovery Programme), which provided aid for drug addicts and alcoholics. The same year she met property developer Rod Weston who became her long-time partner.

Pattie had been taking photographs from the Sixties, but for the past two decades has taken up the craft professionally. On 14 February 2005 she had her first worldwide gallery premier at the San Francisco Exchange. Sixty of her images were displayed at the exhibition and over the years Pattie has taken shots of many celebrities with a portfolio which includes George Harrison, Eric Clapton, Ronnie Wood, Marianne Faithful, Mick Fleetwood, Mick Jagger and B.B. King.

She now lives in the countryside near to London.

[TWENTY-THREE]

The Beatles vs. The Pink Panther

By Bill Harry

*The Beatles and Peter Sellers? Now that's a winning combination!
Here, Bill Harry of Mersey Beat writes about the famed Pink
Panther actor's meetings and dealings with Liverpool's golden sons.*
—L.M.

~

The late Peter Sellers was one of Britain's major screen comedy stars, his most memorable character being the bungling Inspector Clouseau in the 'Pink Panther' films.

Sellers, born on 8 September 1925, first rose to fame in Britain as a member of the Goons, who created an anarchic radio series which ran until 1960. The Goons comprised Peter, along with Spike Milligan, Harry Seacombe and Michael Bentine.

John Lennon was twelve years old when he first heard the Goons and listened avidly to their radio shows until he was sixteen. Their influence was evident in his books *In His Own Write* and *A Spaniard*

In The Works and in 1973 the *New York Times* commissioned John to write a review of the recently published book *The Goon Show Scripts*.

The Goons were also the stars of *The Running, Jumping and Standing Still Film*, directed by Dick Lester, who went on to direct the Beatles movies.

George Martin originally recorded Sellers, producing an album called *Songs For Swinging Sellers*, which proved to be a talking point between George Martin and the Beatles when he first began recording them.

Martin also produced the singles "Goodness Gracious Me" and "Bangers And Mash", duets between Sellers and Sophia Loren, both of which entered the British charts.

It was Peter who presented the Beatles with their Grammy Award at Twickenham Studios on Wednesday 28 April 1965. The National Academy of Recording Arts and Sciences had given the award for "A Hard Day's Night" as the 'Best Performance of a Vocal Group' for the year 1964. When presenting the Grammy, Sellers referred to it as the 'Grandma Award.' The presentation was filmed and a clip appeared on the NBC Grammy Awards programme *The Best of Record* on Tuesday 18 May 1965.

Incidentally, the presentation was made on the studio set of *Help!* and, interestingly, Sellers had originally been offered the script of *Help!* (Obviously under a different title) but turned it down.

Sellers appeared as a guest of the Beatles on the Granada television special 'The Music of Lennon & McCartney' in which he dressed as Richard III and performed a cod Shakespearean rendition of "A Hard Day's Night." His single of the number was issued on Parlophone R 5393 and reached No. 14 in the British charts in December 1965.

In the film *The Magic Christian*, Sellers appeared as Sir Guy Grand and Ringo portrayed Sellers' adopted son, Youngman Grand. Margaret Tarrant, in *Films and Filming*, wrote: "The surreal world of the Goons and the picaresque fantasy world of the Beatles are combined in an essentially genial indictment of British capitalist society," while another reviewer wrote: "Ringo Starr continues to exploit the melancholy wanderer's role he made his own in *A Hard Day's Night*."

Ringo's part had been specially written for the film (the character he played wasn't in the original book), and his role was mainly that of an observer, watching the various stunts which Sellers sets up.

Peter Sellers and Ringo Starr became close friends during the making of the film and used to play practical jokes such as knotting together the belts of coats belonging to the film crew. When one of Ringo's friends visited the set he couldn't figure out why there were so many sniggers, until he discovered that a variety of objects, including match boxes and empty cigarettes packets, had been taped to his back.

When filming was completed the two of them hosted a joint party at the fashionable Les Ambassadeurs in London and John and Yoko and Paul and Linda attended, along with a host of film stars, including George Peppard, Michael Caine, Roger Moore, Richard Harris, Sean Connery, Christopher Lee, Spike Milligan and Stanley Baker. This took place on 4 May 1969 and later that month Sellers joined Ringo, George and their respective wives on the QE2, heading for New York.

Sellers agreed to sell his house Brookfield to Ringo for £70,000, even though he'd recently spend £50,000 on renovating it. John Lennon wanted to buy the house and offered him £150, 000, but Sellers decided to keep his word to Ringo.

While he was negotiating the sale at Brookfield, Ringo noticed a set of drums in the studio there and was told that Peter had started out on his career as a drummer. The fifteenth century oak-beamed house in Elstead, near Guildford in Surrey, had several acres of ground, its own lake, paddocks, walled gardens and barns, a gymnasium, changing rooms, sauna and a private cinema. Ringo was later to sell it to Stephen Stills.

Michael Sellers, Peter Sellers' son, reminiscing in his book *P.S. I Love You* (Collins 1981), mentioned that his father had once ordered a Beatles suit to be specially made for him. His father also revealed that he'd once been asked to invest in the Beatles career before they became famous, but had decided that the £2,000 required was a sum he didn't want to risk at the time. However, he did agree to form a property development business with George Harrison, as they both had Dennis O'Brien acting as their business manager. Sellers, however, lost interest in the company because things seemed to be taking so much time, so he resigned his directorship.

Sellers used to visit George Harrison at Friar Park and had been introduced to Ravi Shankar by the Beatles. He was affected by George's philosophy for a time and began to wear kaftans, practice yoga, chant, burn incense and eat macrobiotic food.

Sellers had given Ravi Shankar financial support early in their relationship and became disenchanted when, on asking if Ravi could perform a recital for some friends, was quoted a huge fee for the short evening's entertainment.

During the recording of The Beatles' double album, there was a degree of tension between the individual members. On Thursday 22 August 1968, Paul made a comment to Ringo that he'd fluffed while playing a tom-tom. Ringo walked out of the sessions threatening to quit. He spent the next fortnight on a yacht in the Mediterranean owned by Sellers and while there he penned the number 'Octopus's Garden.'

At one time Peter Sellers dropped into Apple and was taped having a bizarre chat with the Beatles:

Lennon: "Now, what do you think about Mock Tudor shit-houses in Weybridge and places like that?"
Ringo: "I don't mind them being in Weybridge—it's just when they try and put them in London, they get in the way of the traffic."
Lennon: "As you said yesterday, neither your arse nor your elbow."
Ringo: "I said that?"
Lennon: "I'll never forget it . . .Pull up a star's seat. We've been lucky enough this evening to secure the talents of Mr. Peter Sellers here, who is going to give us Number Three."

Sellers: "Number Three, folks, Number Three."

Lennon: "How about that, folks? That was Number Three from Peter Sellers. Now on to the next round."

Sellers: "And there's more where that came from."

Lennon: "If I ask him really nicely he'll probably do Number Five."

Sellers: "Yes, I might."

Lennon: "Over to you Peter."

Ringo: "Is he doing Number Five?"

Sellers: "I can't count that far these days. I used to be able to."

Lennon: "Do you remember when I gave you that grass in Piccadilly?"

Sellers: "Really stoned me out of my mind, really. Acapulco Gold, wasn't it? Fantastic!"

Lennon: "Exactly."

Sellers: "Sorry I'm not holding any right now."

Lennon: "We can't get it."

Sellers: "Oh, yeah?"

Lennon: "I've given up, you know—as stated by Unter Damn Yer (Hunter Davies)."

Sellers: "Well, I'm sorry about that, fellas, but I, you know, if I'd known I was going to see you, of course, I would have had some on me. Because I know how you love it and dig chewing that thing."

McCartney: Got you, Pete. You got it? Can you dig it?"

Sellers: "Oh yes, God, I can dig it."

Lennon: "Do you want to make the scene in the gents' lavatory?"

Sellers: "That's a groove."

Lennon: "Way out."

Sellers: "Exit?"

Lennon: "Just don't leave the needles lying around, you know. We've got a bad reputation."

Ringo appeared with Sellers and Spike Milligan on London Weekend Television's 'Frost on Saturday' show on 6 December 1969.

Sellers' version of 'She Loves You', originally recorded in 1965, was finally released posthumously in 1981.

Peter Sellers died of a heart attack on 24 July 1980.

~

"Peter Sellers and the Beatles," Bill Harry. Originally published in Mersey Beat. Copyright Bill Harry

[TWENTY-FOUR]

Good Ol' Freda

By Marsha Lederman

If you want to learn the Beatles' dirty secrets, who better to talk to than their secretary? Freda Kelly is a name that's only recently been appearing in Beatles circles as she previously has kept fairly silent about her history with the Fab Four. Now she's opened up to disclose a rich history of warmth and friendship with our heroes.—L.M.

In a 1963 Christmas message recorded for their fans, the Beatles goof around, making jokes and singing *Good King Wenceslas*, before George Harrison pipes up about an integral member of their operation. "Nobody else has said anything yet about our secretary, Freda Kelly, in Liverpool," he says, after which his bandmates chime in: "Good ol' Freda."

For 50 years, Good ol' Freda has kept quiet about her time with the band, rejecting numerous opportunities to satisfy the hunger for insider Beatle info. But when life circumstances led to a change of heart, she approached a family friend who she knew made documentaries. Los Angeles-based Ryan White was skeptical, and surprised. To him, Kelly was his aunt's friend who was working as a secretary at a law firm. Yes, in Liverpool—but the Beatles?

At first, "I thought maybe Freda worked for the Beatles for a few months or something, cashing in. I had no idea the scope with which she worked for them," says White, 31. "But we began having phone calls across the pond and she would just start telling me stories, and I was sort of immediately blown away."

The result of their collaboration, *Good Ol' Freda*—shown at this year's Hot Docs festival in Toronto, and closing the DOXA Documentary Film Festival in Vancouver this weekend—is packed with history, including archival photographs, many of which had been sitting in Kelly's attic for decades, tucked behind the Christmas decorations. The film's appeal isn't just its inner-circle vantage point, but the low-key, matter-of-fact Liverpudlian charm of the woman who provides it. "I was just a secretary then, and funny enough I'm still a secretary now," says Kelly in the film. "And who would want to hear a secretary's story?"

Kelly worked for the Beatles for 11 years—she was with the band longer than they were a band—hired by Brian Epstein in 1962 before Beatlemania exploded, and running their fan club even after they disbanded.

She met Epstein and the band because she was a dedicated fan—but not an over-the-top fanatic. Secretary by day, she initially ran the fan club out of her home. Her monthly dispatches for the Beatles mailouts, signed "Tarrah For Now, Freda Kelly," ranged from innocuous updates about George Harrison's dental work to a full-on finger-wagging at fans who had the audacity to judge the band members' private lives.

"She has a killer memory," White says. If Kelly was unsure about even the tiniest detail about something, she would refuse to tell the story. So what audiences do hear, he says, is "absolutely 100-percent the truth."

Ever the professional, Kelly, who kept big secrets for the Beatles when she was working for them, refuses to dish dirt—as she has all these years, even when a newspaper reporter tried to bribe her. "I'm not prepared to sell me soul to the devil for a few pounds," she says in the film.

But the stories she does tell are evocative, especially of the band's early days. Kelly talks about going around to Ringo Starr's mother's house to instruct her on how to answer the drummer's fan mail, and of forming a close bond with the woman, who eventually went to bat for Kelly and won her a raise.

There's also a story about the time John Lennon fired her for spending too much time in the Moody Blues' dressing room across the hall before a performance. Kelly, maybe a little tipsy, turned the situation around, and for a moment, she was boss. "I'll tell you what: Get down on your two knees and beg me to come back, then . . . and he did."

The stories, says White, were so unrehearsed because Kelly had never told them before. Even her daughter was surprised after attending the world premiere at South by Southwest in March. "She came up to me at the afterparty and said that 95 per cent of that film was completely new to her," White recalls.

Kelly's silence on the subject changed when her daughter had a son a few years after the death of Kelly's own son. She wanted her grandson to be proud of her and to know that she wasn't always just, as she puts it, an old lady with grey hair, sitting in the corner.

Says White, "The fact that she can hand him a DVD one day and he'll understand the crazy decade that she had when she was a teenager, *that* she was very pleased with. . . . If the film completely bombed and no one ever saw it, I don't think she would care." That does not appear to be a concern. *Good Ol' Freda* has been picked up by Magnolia for distribution and is expected to have a theatrical release this year.

After Kelly wrapped up the fan club to concentrate on raising her children, she had nothing to do with the Beatles any more. She stayed in touch with her Beatles family, and has mourned many deaths; but mostly they've all gone their separate ways.

"She's a regular secretary in Liverpool and not rich and famous," says White, "and they are the most rich and famous people in the world."

≈

[TWENTY-FIVE]

The Plastic Ono Band

By Tristin Hopper

By 1969, the Beatles were almost at their breaking point. Both Ringo and George had walked out during recording sessions and nearly left the group; each of the Fab Four was pulling away in his own direction. However, it was John who was drifting more than the others. Gradually, the founder of the Beatles came to be the "Anti-Beatle" who would eventually proclaim "I don't believe in Beatles." John's stint in Canada with his own "Plastic Ono Band" supergroup was a sign of the major divide that would split the most famous rock band of all time. —L.M.

~

In August of 1966, the Beatles had just arrived in Toronto for a pair of appearances at Maple Leaf Gardens that, unbeknownst to the world, would be among their last. Prior to the shows, in a press conference at the arena's Hot Stove Lounge, a reporter asked John Lennon if the band—who had failed to sell out the 16,000-seat venue—would ever split up.

"We obviously are not going to go around holding hands forever," he replied, eliciting laughter from the assembled press.

Lennon added, more seriously, "we've got to split up or progress . . . it might happen. It's quite possible."

The Toronto reporters could not have known, but by the end of the decade, their budding metropolis would soon become the catalyst for the destruction of the greatest band of all time.

In September, 1969, a very different John Lennon stepped into the arrivals lounge at Toronto International Airport.

The 28-year-old had traded his moptop for long hair and a bushy beard, he had married a Japanese artist seven years his senior and the Beatles were now barely on speaking terms.

Lennon himself had grown particularly disillusioned with the Fab Four. He had been showing up to recording sessions blasted on drugs, he had lambasted Paul McCartney's contributions to the album *Abbey Road* as "granny music" and he had begun to openly resent the Beatles' entire rise to fame as a colossal sellout.

"It's torture every time we produce anything. The Beatles haven't got any magic you haven't got. We suffer like hell anytime we make anything," he would tell music columnist Howard Smith in a Canadian interview.

Although Lennon had been in Canada only two months prior for his famous Montreal Bed-in, he had been brought back by the gutsy invitation of Toronto concert promoter John Brower.

Mr. Brower's Toronto Rock and Roll Revival, to be held at Varsity Stadium, had originally been planned as revue of 1950s rock and roll stars, and he had attracted a lineup including Jerry Lee Lewis, Chuck Berry and modern acts such as Alice Cooper and The Doors. But amid lacklustre ticket sales and the threat of cancellation, Mr. Brower had called up the London headquarters of Apple Corps hoping to attract Lennon, a well-known fan of Berry and another '50s rocker on the bill, Gene Vincent. The plan was for Lennon and wife Yoko Ono to appear merely as emcees, but the restless Beatle shot back that he would only appear if he could perform with a hastily cobbled together non-Beatles group he soon dubbed the Plastic Ono Band.

Mr. Brower had struck the jackpot, and he quickly arranged plane tickets and got the group's border papers in order. But still, the idea of a Beatle playing an impulsive show in Canada was so unbelievable that Toronto's CHUM radio refused to broadcast Lennon's pending appearance, thinking it was a hoax.

Only when Torontonians saw Lennon being escorted to Varsity Stadium by a protective motorcade of the Toronto Vagabonds motorcycle gang, did word leak out.

Surprisingly, Lennon was frightened at the prospect of a stadium full of Canadians. Lennon had not performed to a large audience in three years, and his band's only rehearsal had been conducted in the back of the Boeing 707 that had taken them to Toronto.

"I just threw up for hours until I went on . . . I could hardly sing," Lennon would say later.

An awestruck crowd greeted the group just after midnight. Not only was it Lennon's first major performance without George, Paul or Ringo at his side, but he had brought along English guitar god Eric Clapton and future Yes drummer Alan White.

Almost as soon as the band kicked off with a series of 1950s rock and roll standards, though, the crowd soon found that the performance was to be punctuated by the incessant high-pitched screeching of Yoko Ono.

First, she shrieked over renditions of Yer Blues and Cold Turkey, during which she retreated into a tent-like sack on stage.

Then, for 17 straight minutes, she shrieked through a freeform song later identified as "Don't Worry Kyoko (Mummy's only looking for her hand in the snow) / John, John (Let's hope for peace)."

"I did an improvisation," Ms. Ono would tell the National Post in 2000. "I was never exposed to a huge audience like that. I was dazed."

The Toronto crowd soon began to turn. Witnesses remembered booing, obscenities and even the occasional projectile directed at Ms. Ono.

Canadian rocker Ronnie Hawkins, who would take Lennon snowmobiling at his Ontario estate that winter, did not mince words in his 1989 autobiography.

"As hip as everyone there tried to be, Yoko was too much," he wrote. "'Get the f— off the stage,' people started to scream."

To this day, a live album of the concert, *Live Peace in Toronto*, continues to alienate even the most die-hard Beatles fans with its notoriously shriek-filled B-side. "This is excruciating pain, both for listeners and for Ono," reads an otherwise positive Amazon.com review.

All of this was lost on Lennon, who found the experience intoxicating.

"The buzz was incredible," he told a British music magazine soon after returning to the U.K. "I never felt so good in all my life. Everybody was with us and leaping up and down doing the peace sign."

It was a taste of solo life and, in the words of rock writer Ritchie Yorke, who had covered the Toronto concert, Lennon had discovered that there was "life beyond the Beatles."

Breaking up the Beatles was not a new idea. Ringo Starr had threatened to leave during the sessions for *Sgt. Pepper's Lonely Hearts Club Band*, and earlier in 1969, George Harrison had temporarily quit by storming out of a recording session in a huff.

Lennon had been contemplating leaving since 1966, but he later said he could "never step out of the palace because it was too frightening."

But only hours after facing 25,000 people in Toronto, a newly emboldened Lennon returned to London determined to finally bury the Beatles once and for all. Those around him said that after his Canada trip, Lennon had become instilled with the euphoria of a new divorcee.

It would be months before the public would learn of the breakup via a press release from Paul McCartney, but in the *Beatles Anthology*, released in 2000, Ringo Starr himself gave Toronto due credit for the band's demise.

"After the Plastic Ono Band's debut in Toronto we had a meeting in Savile Row where John finally brought it to its head. He said, 'Well, that's it lads. Let's end it.' And we all said 'Yes.'"

[TWENTY-SIX]

Is Paul Dead?

By Harry Castleman and Walter J. Podrazik

The end of Beatles touring left a void in fans' hearts that they had to fill with something—even if that something was wild conspiracy theories. In this famous case, the theory that Paul McCartney died and was replaced with a look-alike known at different times and by different people as Billy Shears, William Shears Campbell, and Faul (you know, "Fake" Paul). Clues are scattered throughout the Beatles' albums and Sgt. Pepper is a particular treasure trove. Harry Castleman and Walter J. Podrazik, two highly prominent Beatles' experts with several books under their belt, here give us a superior overview of the chilling "Paul is Dead" urban legend from their book The Beatles Again?, the second of three volumes in the Harry Castleman/Walter J. Podrazik discography guide to the group's records. (All Together Now; The Beatles Again?; The End of The Beatles?). Information on Watching TV, the latest book by Harry Castleman and Walter J. Podrazik, can be found at watchingtv.org. —L.M.

Question: Is Paul Dead?

Answer: Yes . . . ha! Just kidding. "But seriously folks . . . " Voted the most tiresome, over asked question of the decade, this whole "mystery" seems unwilling to completely die out even after eight years. Being *extremely* tired of the entire matter, we'll try to clear it up as quickly as possible.

In late 1969 around the time of *Abbey Road*'s release (and as the Beatles were breaking up) a rumor, apparently starting in a mid-west radio station, that Paul McCartney was dead swept the country. Not just suddenly dead, but dead for up to three years. The Beatles had stopped touring in August 1966 and had been relatively inaccessible ever since. The idea of Paul being dead seemed oddly appealing. It allowed for a much more "acceptable" explanation for the disintegration of one of the central forces of the 1960s, much like the real, tangible desire many people feel for a link between the Kennedy and King assassinations. Many people find the random nature of life unacceptable, rejecting the fact that many things said and done by people in the public eye mean either nothing or nothing understandable outside of a small circle of friends (i.e., an inside joke). Infusing diverse objects like a random photograph or a doggerel song with "hidden" inner meanings bestows superhuman attributes to the artist/idol, while at the same time allowing the average fan to feel a personal kinship by being able to "figure it out."

Within a month of the rumor's start, an elaborate concordance had been unearthed by various amateur archaeologists, beginning with the *Sgt. Pepper* album in 1967, the first album released after the Beatles stopped touring. The detailed cover of *Sgt. Pepper* showed a gathering around a grave with flowers in the shape of a guitar (was it Paul they were burying?). The character behind Paul has his palm outstretched above McCartney's head, said to be the traditional Norse symbol of death. The inside pictures showed Paul with a shoulder patch which apparently said "O.P.D.", a common abbreviation for "Officially Pronounced Dead." The back cover picture of the four Beatles had John, George, and Ringo facing the camera, but Paul (mysteriously) showing only his back, and (wait! There's more!) George is pointing to the phrase, "Wednesday Morning at Five O'Clock" on the lyrics layered over the Beatles' picture (this supposedly referred to the time of day Paul was involved in a fatal or crippling car crash). This car crash was the most commonly accepted cause of Paul's disappearance. To replace him, the story goes, the Beatles took in the winner of the Paul McCartney look-alike contest (perhaps the mysterious Billy Shears referred to in the title song).

The November 1967 album *Magical Mystery Tour* was chockablock full of prospective clues. If you held the album cover up to a mirror, a phone number is said to be visible in the design of the word *Beatles.* If an intrepid American were to call this number with the correct London prefix and at the right time, the one-and-only Billy Shears (himself) would give explicit directions toward Pepperland, the paradise-on-earth depicted in the movie *Yellow Submarine.* This may all sound absurd now, but at the time it was gospel. A caller to an all-night radio show on the topic fervently explained that three of his friends had recently called the number and vanished! What was in Pepperland was never quite clear. Perhaps it was Paul McCartney living out a tortured existence as a crippled vegetable. (Who knows, maybe along with Jack Kennedy and Marilyn Monroe?) Inside the *Magical Mystery Tour* album were numerous stills from the Beatles' film of the same name (*never* seen in the U.S. at that time, please note). One photo showed all four in white tuxedos. All but Paul had red carnations on their lapels; Paul's was black, signifying *death*! At the very end of the fade of "Strawberry Fields Forever," a previous single tacked onto the American album, John mumbles a line said to be "I buried Paul" which John later claimed was "cranberry sauce," which also sounds like "I'm very bored" (an apt statement in regards to such nit-picking). Featured extensively on the album is the image and notion of the walrus, signifying . . . well, that never was made clear.

The November 1968 *Beatles* double album (the "White Album") had John "confirming" that Paul *was* the walrus, later recanted in his solo song "God." Much more confusing was the track labeled "Revolution No. 9"—an eight-minute mélange of sound effects and tape loops mainly devised by John. It was radically different from anything the Beatles had put on record before. Actually just part of a newly developing interest John was showing in esoterica in general (see his and Yoko's *Two Virgins* album), "Revolution No. 9" was poured over, played backwards, separated and analyzed. The fact that the beginning of EMI test tape number nine, unfortunately sounding like John, was repeated over and over and seemed to say "Turn me on Deadman" when played backwards was the final nail in the coffin (sorry) for many people. "Revolution No. 9" was seen as a story in sound of Paul's car crash, incineration and death. Inasmuch as Lennon threw in so many spur-of-the-moment ideas, "Revolution No. 9" was the perfect choice into which anyone could read anything they chose.

Finally (thank goodness) came *Abbey Road*, with its famous cover. The four Beatles were said to be symbolizing a funeral procession: John, resplendent in white, would be the preacher. George, in work shirt and blue jeans, would be the gravedigger. Ringo, in black, would be in mourning. And Paul, seemingly out of step with the others, would be dead (he alone was barefoot). True enthusiasts, unaware of the British license plate system, interpreted the Volkswagen plate "28IF" as a reference to how old Paul would be "if he had lived."

Such clues (and *many, many* others of the more obscure variety) were batted about and put to unbelieving English executives and friends by scoop-hungry American DJs. Some enterprising soul even collected the main clues, put a backbeat behind it, and released a record on MGM called "The Ballad of Paul." Paul, as it turned out, happened to be incommunicado on his new Scottish farm. With the 1970 release of his first solo album, and the birth of his first child, the rumors died down.

Aside from marking the first "Bring Back The Beatles" hysteria, the whole "Paul Is Dead" affair was the ultimate limit of insane fandom. Granted, most Beatles songs say *something*, but much, if not all, of the surrounding ephemera (i.e. cover work and photos) are, and always have been, spurious momentary decisions containing nothing more intense than an occasional private joke. To a generation getting ready to proclaim the Beatles as prophets (a role they never asked for), such light-heartedness was the ultimate, unacceptable crime.

Nonetheless, old rumors never die . . . say, where is Judge Crater?

∾

[TWENTY-SEVEN]

Harrison's All Things Must Pass

By Randy Lewis

Discussions about the Beatles' legacy tends to center around
Lennon/McCartney. But in the final analysis, it would be unjust
not to make strong mention of George's immense (and often
undervalued) genius, which is perhaps nowhere more apparent
than in the grandness of his first solo album. —L.M.

What kind of contrarian would single out 1970 as his favorite year
for Beatles music? That was, after all, the year the Beatles disbanded
and broke the hearts of millions around the world.

"We got something like 14 Beatles records that year: Not only
the *Hey Jude* and *Let it Be* (Beatles) albums, but solo albums from
Paul, George, John and two from Ringo, plus John's "Instant Karma"
single, "My Sweet Lord" from George, etc. So it really is my favorite
year," said Chris Carter, host of the long-running "Breakfast With the
Beatles" radio show heard Sunday mornings at 9 a.m. in Los Angeles

on KLOS-FM (95.5). It certainly was a year of dramatic transition
for all four Beatles as the group that brought so many innovations
to pop music during its eight-year recording career called it quits,
and each member of the quartet moved forward with solo endeav-
ors. The biggest surprise of all, however, may have been Harrison's
emergence from the long shadow of Lennon and McCartney with
his first post-Beatles solo release in the triple album *All Things Must
Pass*. It came out in the U.S. 45 years ago, on Nov. 27, 1970.

"In my opinion—and I've called it this on the air—it's a complete
masterpiece," said Les Perry, host of Southern California's other
weekly Beatles broadcast, "Saturday With the Beatles," which airs
Saturdays at 10 a.m. on KCSN-FM (88.5).

"I was working at (LA radio station) KDAY in the music department when that came out," Perry said. "It was an event. It was this
(physically) big album, it had a great poster of George inside, and
everybody wanted it. We (programmed) two songs right away, that
afternoon: 'My Sweet Lord' and 'What Is Life.' There wasn't one bad
song on it."

"Breakfast With the Beatles" and "Saturday With the Beatles"
will include spotlights on Harrison's music in general and *All Things
Must Pass* in particular during this weekend's broadcasts.

Carter, as one of the world's foremost authorities on *All Things
Must Pass*, has amassed a collection of dozens of versions of the full
album as well as promotional posters, the original singles and more
recent vintage CD reissues.

Part of Carter's *All Things Must Pass* collection is a multi-platinum
RIAA award certification created in 2001 after the 30th-anniversary
reissue, which Harrison was involved with during the final year of his
life. Carter was given the plaque for his contributions of liner notes
and memorabilia that went into the 30-year anniversary reissue of
All Things Must Pass in 2000.

The original version, Carter noted, "came out when I was 11 years
old, and it was really my first 'grown-up' record purchase," he said
at his home studio in Los Angeles' Sherman Oaks neighborhood.
"It came in a box, so it looked like a classical album, and even at 11

I could tell the music was different, more grown-up, than other things I'd been listening to."

Carter remains an ardent devotee of the powerful musical statement Harrison made with *All Things Must Pass*, containing several songs written for but rejected by the Beatles for latter-day albums such as *The Beatles* (aka the White Album), *Abbey Road* and *Let it Be*. (Lennon and McCartney reportedly gave him thumbs down on the songs "All Things Must Pass" and "Hear Me Lord" as they were recording what would become the *Let it Be* album.)

He has noted on his radio show Harrison's not-so-subtle dig at his former band mates by positioning "I'd Have You Anytime" as the leadoff track for *All Things Must Pass*. He wrote with no less than Bob Dylan, and Carter thinks "that was George's way of telling John and Paul, 'Bob Dylan seems to think I'm a decent enough songwriter.'"

Said Perry, "I think there is a big, big Bob Dylan influence on that album. The style that George used in his lyrics—even the ones that weren't written by Bob had that influence."

Among its other milestone accomplishments, *All Things Must Pass* yielded the first No. 1 single from a solo Beatle: "My Sweet Lord," which topped the Billboard Hot 100 for four weeks and stayed on the chart for almost four months. A second single, "What Is Life," made the Top 10 the following February.

It also features songs addressing mortality ("Art of Dying," which he'd written in 1966), the politics of religion ("Awaiting on You All"), philosophy ("Beware of Darkness," the title track) and the ups and downs of love ("I Dig Love," "Isn't It a Pity").

"I don't think there's a week that goes by that I don't play something from *All Things Must Pass* on the show," Carter said. "I even like the 'Apple Jam' disc," referring to the third part of the three-LP album containing largely instrumental jams among Harrison and his superstar pals including Eric Clapton, Ringo Starr, Leon Russell, Billy Preston, Dave Mason and numerous others.

Carter also has been touched by the spirit of Harrison's music and his family.

"One time I got a call from (Harrison's widow) Olivia, and she called to thank me for playing George's music," Carter said of a show entirely dedicated to Harrison's songs—with the Beatles and solo. "Her mother still lives here (in Southern California) and told her she'd heard it. Olivia was calling from their estate in Friar Park (in Britain), and she said it was raining, and she talked about how George loved the rain and he would always go out into the garden and plant something when it rained.

"I'm sitting here in Los Angeles, where the sun is shining and thinking, 'She took the time to call me just to say thank you for playing her husband's music,'" he said.

"That shows you what kind of people they are."

∿

"George Harrison's 'All Things Must Pass' still inspires 45 years later," Randy Lewis. Licensed from Los Angeles Times. © 2015 Los Angeles Times. All Rights Reserved. iCopyright license: 3.16844-41202.

[TWENTY-EIGHT]

Muhammad Ali Tries to Reunite the Beatles

By Steve Politi

The Beatles met Muhammad Ali in 1964. They were fairly unknown to each other in that first encounter, with Ali famously asking afterward "who were those little sissies?" But that didn't stop them from making a good photoshoot. It seems that Ali had become musically educated by the late '70s because he was the force behind an effort to bring the broken band back together. For more on Ali, check out Fighting Words: The Greatest Muhammad Ali Stories Ever Told from FanReads. —L.M.

∾

He tells the story now, even 40 years later, with a profound sense of awe. Joel Sacher was attending the inauguration gala for President Jimmy Carter, which would have represented a life milestone for the longtime Springfield resident regardless of the circumstances. But he was there as a personal guest of Muhammad Ali, maybe the most recognizable man on the planet at the time. And we use the word *maybe* here for a reason.

Because Ali and Sacher were meeting with one of the few men who could challenge for that distinction. They were talking to John Lennon and his wife Yoko Ono, and while the conversation included plenty of nostalgia about a famous meeting between a band and a boxer long ago, it was more than just reliving the good old days.

Ali was armed with a proposal, one that was the brainchild of Sacher and a business associate that had the potential to stun the world. They wanted to reunite the most famous quartet in rock 'n' roll history, and do so for the benefit of impoverished people around the globe.

They weren't the first to try to bring the Fab Four back together, of course, against daunting odds. The lads from Liverpool had not parted as the closest of friends when they had broken up seven years earlier.

Still: Sacher remembers an overwhelming feeling of hope that night in January 1977, and for good reason. He had a very convincing ally, after all.

"If there was anybody in the world who could have pulled this off and reunited the Beatles," he told NJ Advance Media this week, "it was Muhammad Ali."

There are hundreds of ways to remember Ali, who will be memorialized in public services in his hometown of Louisville, Kent., on Thursday and Friday.

He was a great boxer, of course—The Greatest, as he himself proclaimed—who won the heavyweight championship three times and lost just five times in 61 fights. He was a showman who, more than any athlete before or since, understood how to turn a sporting event into a spectacle. He was a conscientious objector to the Vietnam War, and as polarizing an icon to ever emerge from the sports world, and a man who courageously lived with Parkinson's Disease and campaigned for research to fight it even as it left him unable to speak. He was all that and more, someone who lived such a big live that something as fascinating as this—his relationship with the world's most famous rock band—is but a footnote. And his attempts to reunite that band near the end of his boxing career? Almost completely lost to history.

Sacher was a witness to it. It started with a chance meeting between Alan Amron, his partner in the effort, in a Miami restaurant early one morning in 1976. Amron was many things—an inventor, a businessman and a promoter—but he certainly wasn't shy.

"Excuse me, sir," he began, according to a recent interview with the Broward-Palm Beach New Times, "but I'm trying to re-form the Beatles. Would you like to help?"

"The Beatles?" Ali replied. "I love the Beatles!"

Ali gave Amron his business card. Soon, according to Sacher, he and his partner were flying to meet the champ in Houston, where he was filming scenes for his movie "The Greatest."

Sacher had grown up idolizing Ali, and now there he was, standing next to him on a movie set. He said he could only stand silently and stare until Ali turned to him and broke the ice.

"What's the matter with you?" he said. "Never seen a black man before?"

That introduction was the beginning of a 40-year friendship. Sacher isn't exactly sure why Ali took such a liking to him, but he has a collection of old photographs and funny stories as proof.

Like the time Ali asked Sacher's kids to make a paper mache acorn, one that his entourage carried around the ring before his fight against Earnie Shavers—who Ali had nicknamed "The Acorn" because of his bald head—in September 1977. Or the time Ali carried his young daughter into a hospital when she was suffering from a urinary tract invention, much to the stunned amazement of the doctors and nurses inside.

"After we met in Texas, Ali had my number and called my house," Sacher said. "My wife answered the phone. He said, 'May I speak to Joel?' She said, 'Who's calling?' He said, 'Muhammad Ali.' And she said, 'Yeah, okay, Joel.' When we met in Philadelphia, Ali said,

'Man, your wife did not believe it was me.' I told him, 'Muhammad, sometimes I don't believe it either.'"

That meeting in Philadelphia, like many others during the late '70s, had a singular focus: Reuniting the Beatles.

They had intersected in history before, of course. This was 1964, soon after the Beatles made their famous appearance on *The Ed Sullivan Show*. They wanted to meet Sonny Liston, but the heavyweight champ refused, so the band's management set something up with his underdog opponent—still known as Cassius Clay then—in the much-anticipated upcoming title bout.

It was Feb. 18, 1964, when the band arrived at Miami Beach's 5th Street Gym. Both sides were skeptical, according to observers at the time, but the musicians soon found a match to their comedic instincts in the boxer. They took a series of iconic photographs, including one in which Ali picked up drummer Ringo Starr.

"And then he's carrying me. I don't know why, he just picked me up!" Starr told Rolling Stone in an interview this week. "It wasn't like, 'OK, pick him up now!' He just suddenly did."

That they would all go onto fame that would transcend boxing and music made that moment—and those photos—something of a cultural touchstone. Ali never forgot it, even if the boxer and the band would only cross paths a few times after that meeting.

Flash forward to 1977. Sacher and Amron knew that it would take more than money to bring the Beatles back together. It would take a cause. It would take a movement. They hatched a plan for an event that could raise $200 million to create a permanent agency that focused on "feeding and clothing the poor people of the world."

Ali's representatives reached out to the lawyers for the four Beatles, with limited success. Then, on Jan. 15, 1977, Ali took the story public with an interview with New York tabloid the Daily News.

The headline on the front page that day: "Ali to Beatles: Come Together." The story made it clear that no one involved wanted to profit on the venture except for the good of humanity.

"I don't need the money and neither do the Beatles." Ali told the newspaper. "The idea is to create this fund, and to help people to develop a quality of the heart."

Sacher is mentioned briefly near the bottom of the story as, along with Armon, "the catalysts" for the effort and for forming the "International Committee to Reunite the Beatles." But make no mistake: This was all about Ali.

"It would be a personal joy to see them together again," Ali said. "The man who helps unite the Beatles makes a better contribution to human happiness than an astronomer who discovers a new star."

The story, not surprisingly, took off. Sacher found himself taking phone calls from reporters from all over the world. But only one thing mattered: How would the Beatles respond?

Just five days later, at the inaugural gala for Jimmy Carter, he thought he had his answer.

The gala was, in every way, a spectacle. Linda Ronstadt sang "crazy." John Wayne delivered a speech, telling the new president, "Starting tomorrow at high noon, all of our hopes and dreams go into that great house with you." Lauren Bacall was there. Paul Newman was there.

And so was Joel Sacher, feeling like he had stepped in as an extra in some unbelievable movie. He was with Ali when the boxer approached Lennon, wearing a tuxedo with a star lapel pin, and struck up a conversation.

"Yoko and John were so enamored with Ali," Sacher said. "They were more excited about seeing him than the President. It brought back such memories for them, they couldn't stop talking about having met him in '64 and all that had transpired in the world since then. It was a moment in time you could never recreate."

Ali wasn't going to secure a commitment from Lennon that night. But he did earn an invitation. Come meet with us, Lennon told Ali, at their famed apartment at The Dakota and we'll talk some more.

A meeting? It was a start.

"Ali and I left like two little boys," Sacher said. "We were so obviously thrilled I can't tell you. We just kept looking at each other. This would have been a victory bigger than any of his fights. Here he was champion of the world in the ring, and now he would have been champion in the world of promotions!"

Alas, it didn't happen that way. Geraldo Rivera had gotten involved, Sacher said, and in an interview with the TV newsman Paul McCartney—who was atop the charts with his new band "Wings" in early 1977—made it pretty clear. He wouldn't say no, but not even the champ was likely to make this reunion happen.

Sacher said there were many behind-the-scenes meetings with representatives from the musician and the boxer over the coming months, but they never did have that sit down at The Dakota. It was outside that building, on Dec. 8, 1980, when an assassin's bullet ended their dreams for good.

Lennon was dead, and with the rest of the world, Ali was grieving.

"Ali was devastated, and not the fact that we couldn't get the Beatles back together, but that another person could take someone life's as such a talented individual," Sacher said. "It had a profound effect on Ali for a while. It had that effect on all of us. Why? Why end a life like that?"

Now the world is grieving again. Sacher will be among the thousands who travel to Louisville this week to pay his respects to Ali. He never lost touch with the boxer, last seeing him in September 2014 when he posed for a photograph with Sacher's entire family.

Ali even playful sparred with his young grandson.

The many tributes to Ali from around the world included words from the two surviving Beatles. Starr tweeted simply: "God bless Muhammad Ali peace and love to all his family."

McCartney, meanwhile, wrote "I loved that man."

"He was great from the first day we met him in Miami, and on the numerous occasions when I ran into him over the years," he wrote on his website. "Besides being the greatest boxer, he was a beautiful, gentle man with a great sense of humour who would often pull a pack of cards out of his pocket, no matter how posh the occasion, and do a card trick for you."

Sacher still believes, had Lennon lived, that Ali would have pulled off the greatest reunion in rock 'n' roll history. Maybe that was wishful thinking, but there is one lesson that Ali spent a lifetime teaching the world.

Never doubt The Greatest.

∾

[TWENTY-NINE]

Killing John Lennon

By Allan J. Mayer, Susan Agrest, Jacob Young

John Lennon's death was also the death of the Beatles. Before John was murdered, there always existed the possibility (and hope among fans) that the band would get together again someday, that they'd put aside their differences for another tour or album. That hope disappeared along with John, for without one of the Fab Four a reunion of three will never be the Beatles. With John's death, the Beatles can henceforth exist only in our hearts. —L.M.

A few weeks after John Lennon was shot by obsessed fan Mark David Chapman, *Newsweek* devoted a special report to the singer, painstakingly tracing the steps of his killer and describing the mourning that followed the Dec. 8, 1980 shooting of the beloved Beatle. Read one of the issue stories, published in the Dec. 22, 1980 issue.

Come together, he had once asked them in a song, and now they came, tens of thousands of them, to share their grief and shock at the news. John Lennon, once the cheeky wit and sardonic soul of the Beatles, whose music had touched a generation and enchanted the world, had been slain on his doorstep by a confused, suicidal young man who had apparently idolized him. Along New York's Central Park West and West 72nd Street, in front of the building where Lennon had lived and died, they stood for hours in tearful vigil, looking to each other and his music for comfort. The scene was repeated in Dallas's Lee Park, at San Francisco's Marina Green, on the Boston Common and in countless other gathering places around the country and the world. Young and old, black and white, they lit candles and softly sang his songs. "All you need is love," they chanted in the rain. "Love is all you need."

As the unofficial leader of the Beatles, Lennon had exerted a numinous influence on the popular culture of the 1960s and 1970s. But in recent years he had been something of a recluse, a refugee from the maelstrom of pop superstardom who had abandoned the recording studio and public life in an effort to devote himself to raising his son Sean, now 5. He emerged from his self-imposed retreat just five months ago, on the eve of his 40th birthday, a man finally at peace with himself, the creative juices once again flowing. He and his wife, Yoko Ono, released their first album in eight years and were putting the finishing touches on a second. He was, as he titled his most popular new song, "Starting Over." "[I'm Only] 40," he said cheerfully. "God willing, there are another 40 years of productivity to go." But as he and Yoko returned home from a late-night session at a recording studio early last week, a 25-year-old doppelgänger named Mark David Chapman popped out of the darkness and shot Lennon.

Distraught: The killing stunned the nation—and much of the world—as nothing had since the political assassinations of the 1960s. "At first, I didn't believe he was really dead," said Chris Backus, one of a thousand mourners who assembled the next day at the ABC entertainment complex in Los Angeles to pay tribute to Lennon. "When I realized it was true, then—bang!—part of my childhood was gone forever." As the news spread, radio stations throughout North America and Europe threw away their play lists and began broadcasting nothing but music by Lennon and the Beatles. Even Radio Moscow devoted 90 minutes to his songs. "The phones started ringing right after the news and they didn't stop all day," reported disc jockey Traver Hulse of KATT-FM in Oklahoma City. "It was like losing a President." Distraught fans also descended on record stores, snapping up virtually every Lennon album available. "It was like they had just been robbed of something," said manager Gary Crawford of Strawberries, a downtown Boston record store. "They wanted to replace that something right away."

The question asked over and over again was why—why had Chapman, a moody unemployed amateur guitar player who lived and worked in the South before moving to Hawaii three years ago, killed a man he was said to have admired for fifteen years? There were no simple answers. Police said Chapman told them of hearing "voices," of having "a good side and a bad side," of being annoyed at the way Lennon scrawled his autograph when Chapman first approached him six hours before the shooting. Friends talked of Chapman's obsessive identification with Lennon—how he used to play Beatles songs constantly on his guitar, how he taped the name "John Lennon" over his own on the ID badge he wore as a maintenance man at a Honolulu condominium, how he emulated Lennon by marrying a Japanese woman several years his senior. And psychologists noted that before taking Lennon's life, Chapman had twice tried to take his own. "He had already tried to kill himself and he was unsuccessful, so he decided to kill Lennon," speculated a forensic psychiatrist in Hawaii. "The homicide was simply a suicide turned backward."

'**Normal Dude**': Chapman had apparently been planning to shoot Lennon for weeks. Late in October he quit his job as a maintenance man and applied to the Honolulu police for a pistol permit. Since he had no criminal record, the permit was granted—and on Oct. 27, he went to J&S Sales, Ltd., in Honolulu and paid $169 for a five-shot Charter Arms .38 special. "Just a normal dude," says J&S manager Tom Grahovac. At about the same time, Chapman called local art dealer Pat Carlson, who had sold him a number of expensive lithographs. He wanted to sell one, he told her, because he needed to raise some money. He also called the employment counselor who had found him the condominium job. "He said to me that he had something really big he was planning to do," she recalled.

A week or so later, Chapman left Honolulu for Atlanta, Ga., where he had grown up and gone to school. He told acquaintances that he was in town to see his father, but he never did. Instead, he dropped in on an old girlfriend and visited his high-school chorus teacher, Madison Short. Though the girlfriend's parents said he seemed depressed, Short recalled him insisting that "he was happy, content with his lot in life." Chapman said nothing about going to New York or seeking out John Lennon. After a few days he returned home to Honolulu, but on Dec. 5 he was off again. His wife, Gloria, had no idea of his plans. "She knew he was going somewhere," Gloria's lawyer, Brook Hart, said, "but she didn't know precisely where."

Boast: He arrived in New York on Saturday, Dec. 6, and checked into a $16.50-a-night room at a YMCA just nine blocks from the Dakota, the elegant, century-old apartment building where Lennon and his family lived. That afternoon, taxi driver Mark Snyder picked up Chapman in his cab. According to Snyder, Chapman boasted that he was Lennon's sound engineer, that he was in the midst of a recording session with him and that he had just learned that Lennon and his long-estranged songwriting partner Paul McCartney were going to make an album together.

The same day, Chapman was seen for the first time loitering near an entrance to the Dakota. No one took much notice, the building is home to a number of celebrities—among them, conductor Leonard Bernstein, actress Lauren Bacall and comedienne Gilda Radner— and sidewalk gawkers are a common sight. Chapman reappeared outside the Dakota on Sunday as well. He also changed hotels on Sunday, moving from the Y to a more comfortable $82-a-day room at the Sheraton Centre farther downtown.

On Monday evening Chapman's and Lennon's paths finally crossed. Once again Chapman had spent the afternoon on the sidewalk outside the Dakota—this time in the company of Paul Goresh, a Beatles fan and amateur photographer from North Arlington, N.J.

Goresh, who was also hoping to catch a glimpse of Lennon, said Chapman struck up a conversation as they waited. "He said he spent the last three days trying to see Lennon and get an autograph," Goresh recalled. At about 5 p.m., Lennon and his wife finally emerged from the building on their way to The Record Plant Studios on West 44th Street. Chapman approached Lennon timidly, holding out a copy of John and Yoko's latest album, "Double Fantasy." Lennon took it and scrawled his signature ("John Lennon 1980") across the cover, while Goresh snapped a picture. Chapman was delighted. "John Lennon signed my album," he exulted to Goresh after the Lennons had left. "Nobody in Hawaii is going to believe me."

The two men remained outside the Dakota for another two hours. When Goresh finally decided to go home, Chapman tried to change his mind. Lennon, he said, "should be home soon and you can get your album signed." Goresh replied that he could get Lennon's autograph another day. "I'd wait," Chapman advised somberly. "You never know if you'll see him again."

The Lennons worked at The Record Plant until 10:30 p.m., mixing the sound for a new single, tentatively titled "Walking on Thin Ice." "We had planned to go out to eat after leaving the recording studio," Yoko said later," but we decided to go straight home instead." Their rented limousine delivered them to the Dakota's 72nd Street entrance at about 10:50 p.m. The limousine could have driven into the entranceway, but it stopped at the curb. Yoko got out first, with John trailing a few steps behind. As he passed under the ornate archway leading to the Dakota's interior courtyard, he heard a voice call out from behind. "Mr. Lennon." He turned to see Chapman crouched 5 feet away gripping his .38 special with both hands. Before Lennon had a chance to react, Chapman opened fire, pumping four bullets into his back and left shoulder. "I'm shot!" Lennon gasped. Leaving a trail of blood behind him, he staggered six steps into the doorman's office, where he collapsed.

Calm: While Yoko cradled her husband's head in her arm, Chapman dropped his gun, and the doorman kicked it away. "Do you know what you just did?" the doorman asked Chapman dazedly. "I just shot John Lennon," came the calm reply.

Summoned by the doorman, police were on the scene within minutes. Chapman waited for them, thumbing through a copy of J.D. Salinger's classic novel of adolescent rebellion, *The Catcher in the Rye*. While two officers frisked and handcuffed him, two others attended to Lennon. "I turned him over," said Patrolman Anthony Palma. "Red is all I saw." Palma turned to a rookie cop, who was on the verge of being sick. "The guy is dying," he said. "Let's get him out of here."

Lennon, semiconscious and bleeding profusely, was placed in the back seat of Officer James Moran's patrol car. "Do you know who you are?" Moran asked him. Lennon couldn't speak. "He moaned and nodded his head as if to say yes," Moran said. While Moran raced Lennon to Roosevelt Hospital fifteen blocks away, Palma followed in his car with Yoko. "Tell me it isn't true, tell me he's all right," she implored him over and over again.

Though doctors pronounced Lennon dead on arrival at Roosevelt, a team of seven surgeons labored desperately to revive him. But his wounds were too severe. There were three holes in his chest, two in his back and two in his left shoulder. "It wasn't possible to resuscitate him by any means," said Dr. Stephen Lynn, the hospital's director of emergency services. "He'd lost 3 to 5 quarts of blood from the gun wounds, about 80 per cent of his blood volume." After working on Lennon for about half an hour, the surgeons gave up, and Lynn went to break the news to Yoko. "Where is my husband?" she asked frantically. "I want to be with my husband. He would want me to be with him. Where is he?" Lynn took a deep breath. "We have very bad news," he told her. "Unfortunately, in spite of our massive efforts, your husband is dead. There was no suffering at the end." Yoko refused to comprehend the message. "Are you saying he is sleeping?" she sobbed.

Accompanied by David Geffen, whose Geffen Records was producing the Lennons' new album, Yoko returned home about midnight. She made three phone calls, to "the three people that John would have wanted to know" —his 17-year-old son by his first marriage, Julian; his aunt, Mimi Smith, who had raised him, and his onetime collaborator, Paul McCartney.

Shrine: As word of the shooting spread throughout the city, a spontaneous vigil began to form outside the Dakota. By 1 a.m., a crowd of nearly a thousand had gathered. They sang Lennon songs, lit candles and turned the building's gate into an impromptu shrine, covering it with flowers and pictures of John and Yoko. Within minutes, news of Lennon's death had been flashed round the world, sparking a public outpouring not seen since John Kennedy was assassinated in 1963. President Carter spoke of the irony that Lennon "died by violence, though he had long campaigned for peace"; President-elect Reagan pronounced it "a great tragedy."

In London, a portrait of the Beatles draped with a floral tribute was placed at the entrance to the Tate Gallery. "We usually do this when a British artist whose work is represented in the Tate dies," a spokesman said. "But we thought John Lennon was a special case." In Lennon's hometown of Liverpool, the lord mayor announced plans to hold a memorial service for him at the city's giant cathedral, and local teen-agers placed wreaths at the parking lot that was once the site of the Cavern club, where the Beatles had gotten their start. In New York, hundreds of thousands of mourners planned to gather for a Sunday afternoon memorial in Central Park, not far from the Dakota.

Of the three other former Beatles, only Ringo Starr came to New York to be with Yoko. George Harrison canceled a recording session and reportedly went into seclusion. And McCartney, who called his ex-partner "a great man who will be sadly missed," said he would mourn Lennon in private.

Yoko also stayed out of sight. Two days after the shooting, she released a poignant statement describing how she told Sean of his father's death. "Now Daddy is part of God," she reported Sean as saying. "I guess when you die you become much more bigger because you're part of everything." Yoko also announced there would be no funeral; after Lennon's body was cremated privately, she invited mourners to participate— "from wherever you are at the time" — in a ten-minute silent vigil on Sunday afternoon. "John loved and prayed for the human race," she said. "Please pray the same for him."

Chapman, meanwhile, was charged with second-degree murder (since New York has abandoned the death penalty, first-degree murder is no longer used as a charge) and ordered to undergo 30 days of extensive psychiatric testing. He was first sent, under heavy guard, to a cell at the city's most famous Bellevue Hospital, where he was placed on a 24-hour "suicide watch." But as fears of a Jack Ruby-style revenge killing grew, officials decided to transport him to the more remote jail on Riker's Island.

Chapman's second court-appointed attorney, Jonathan Marks, who was assigned the case after the accused murderer's first law-yer quit, said his client probably would plead not guilty by reason of insanity. "Obviously, Mark Chapman's mental state is a critical issue in this case," Marks told reporters. "In order to convict, the [prosecution] must show criminal intent."

Though Lennon appealed to people of all ages, races and classes, it was the baby-boom generation, now in its 20s and 30s, that was hardest hit by his murder. "We grew up together," said Julie Cohen, a 27-year-old teacher who was among the 2,000 mourners who gathered at San Francisco's Marina Green last week to honor him. "I felt there must be some way it could not be true, that it must be a mistake." Secretary Christy Lyou, 32, who showed up along with 2,500 others in Dallas's Lee Park for a similar memorial, said: "It's the last nail in the coffin of the '60s."

However keen the sense of loss, those closest to Lennon rejected the notion that his death marked the passing of an era. "We had planned so much together," Yoko said the day her husband was cremated. "We had talked about living until we were 80. We even drew up lists of all the things we could do for all those years. Then, it was all over. But that doesn't mean the message should be over. The music will live on." And with it, so will John Lennon.

◦◦◦

"Death of a Beatle," Allan J. Mayer, Susan Agrest, and Jacob Young.
Licensed from Newsweek. © 2014 Newsweek. All Rights Reserved.
iCopyright license: 3.13280-48370.

[THIRTY]

A Final Bow for George

By Washington Times Staff

George Harrison brought a spiritual aspect to the Beatles that becomes most apparent when his solo work is contrasted with the work of other Beatles. Here we read about George's legacy and the impact he's had on millions of lives. —L.M.

∽

Millions gently weep for George Harrison, who died Thursday in Los Angeles after a three-year battle with cancer. He was 58.

Sly, cerebral and kind-hearted, the "quiet Beatle" also had the inner mettle of working-class English roots and the backbone of an old-fashioned rock 'n' roller. His death marks a pivotal moment for music fans who identify the lead guitarist with decades of youth and creativity.

"He left this world as he lived in it, conscious of God, fearless of death, and at peace, surrounded by family and friends," his wife, Olivia, and son Dhani said in a statement. "He often said, 'Everything else can wait, but the search for God cannot wait,' and 'love one another.'"

Hundreds gathered to sing and reminisce at makeshift shrines here and abroad yesterday, celebrating the life of a meticulous and inventive musician known for complex but graceful songs of spirituality, whimsy and more than one raucous moment. Harrison was also mourned by Queen Elizabeth and President Bush, among other global luminaries.

"He was a great guy, full of love for humanity, but he didn't suffer fools gladly," said his former band mate Paul McCartney. "I loved him like a brother."

"He was a best friend of mine," said Ringo Starr. "We will miss George for his sense of love, his sense of music and his sense of laughter."

Armed with a Gretsch guitar and an appealing voice, Harrison persistently crafted his own musical identity in a world fixated upon hits written by John Lennon, who died in 1980, and Mr. McCartney. Harrison never bought into the teen-age hysteria of the early days, warding off an invasive press and swooning females with wry comments and watchful eyes.

"I'm really quite simple," Harrison wrote in his autobiography. "I stay at home and watch the river flow."

Many credit such serenity with smoothing creative differences among the tempestuous Fab Four as they moved from lovable moptops to profound cultural force throughout the 1960s.

"He was always acting as peacemaker between John and Paul," said Gerry Marsden, who once fronted Gerry and the Pacemakers, another Liverpool group from the mid-'60s.

"He was the major cog in the Beatles. He kept them together probably because of the calming effect he had," noted Alan Williams, who was the Beatles' first manager back in Liverpool where Harrison was born, the war baby of a school bus driver and a housewife.

He was a tough lad with a $6 guitar, pompadour, black trousers and a pair of blue suede shoes in 1958. His life changed the day he met Mr. McCartney on the bus his father drove.

Both joined the Quarrymen, a "skiffle" group headed by Lennon. The three honed their distinctive style in dim local clubs and basement recording sessions under names like Johnny and the Moondogs and the Rainbows.

Under the aegis of manager Brian Epstein and producer George Martin, the cleaned-up, carefully coifed Beatles finally rocketed to success in Europe and the United States with the release of such tunes as "I Want to Hold Your Hand," and the landmark pop film *A Hard Day's Night.*

"Although we always felt that John Lennon was the flashiest and most interesting actor, George could always be relied on to hit the square in the middle and get the line right," recalled Richard Lester, who directed the film.

The Beatles' appearance on *The Ed Sullivan Show* in 1964 before hundreds of swooning "little chickadees" as Sullivan fondly called young female fans has become an icon in the annals of TV culture.

On his 21st birthday that same year, Harrison was unimpressed by success. "I doubt if we'll ever be millionaires," he told the BBC. "We'll probably be all right for a few years."

Even as the band recorded a string of chart-busting love songs and rock anthems, Harrison took the road less traveled. Under the guidance of an Indian guru, Harrison took up transcendental meditation and the thrumming, hypnotic sitar in 1966 using the multistringed instrument to accompany the band and fans on a rhythmic journey through psychedelia and reinvention.

The group traded slick Bond Street suits for sherbet-colored satin uniforms and embarked upon an artistic quest that produced the *Sgt. Pepper's Lonely Hearts Club Band* and *Magical Mystery Tour* albums, both of which showcased an increasingly distinctive Harrison style.

On the final Beatles albums, Harrison's contributions included such songs as "While My Guitar Gently Weeps," "Here Comes the Sun" and "Something," an evocative tune Frank Sinatra once called "the most beautiful love song ever written."

After six meteoric years in the public eye, the Beatles finally broke up in 1970, a moment mourned by fans but crucial for Harrison as he went from sideman to front man with the release of *All Things Must Pass*, a solo album released later that year.

But the life of even a successful musician is complex. Harrison was later sued for plagiarizing "He's So Fine," by the Chiffons, an American girl group, to create his album's No. 1 tune "My Sweet Lord." After 20 years in court, the Chiffons won, and he was fined.

Harrison later parodied that experience in a song, and set his focus on humanitarian causes. In 1971, he banded together high-profile musical pals for an all-star Concert for Bangladesh, raising millions for famine relief. Though it was mired in legal complications, the idea set a precedent for splashy big-name events.

Harrison, the only Beatle to grow up in a two-parent family, married twice. His 1966 union to English model Pattie Boyd lasted a decade before she ran off with his close friend, fellow guitarist Eric Clapton. The two men remained friends and musical collaborators, and gleefully referred to themselves as "ex-husbands-in-law" after Miss Boyd also left Mr. Clapton.

Harrison married Olivia Arias in 1978; the couple had one son, Dhani, and lived for decades in Friar Park, a neglected Gothic mansion west of London. Harrison restored the mansion, planted 45,000 flower bulbs and declared the place to be "like heaven."

In the years to follow, Harrison produced films for the Monty Python comedy troupe, recorded more albums, took up Formula One-style road racing and toured with the Traveling Wilburys, a superstar group that included Bob Dylan.

Nineteen years after Lennon was shot to death by a deranged fan, Harrison was attacked at his home by a knife-wielding intruder. Already struggling with newly diagnosed throat cancer, Harrison was slow to recover but philosophical.

"I had a little throat cancer," he said at the time. "And then I was almost murdered." When his first solo album was reissued earlier this year, Harrison once again showed his simple values.

"My music, it doesn't matter if I did it 20 years ago or if I did it tomorrow. It doesn't go with trends," he said in a news conference. "My trousers don't get wider and tighter every six months. My music just stays what it is, and that's the way I like it."

∽

[THIRTY-ONE]

Idolator of the Beatles

By Craig Sailor

When does appreciation become obsession? Does this Tacoma, Washington resident cross the line? —L.M.

The home of Johnny Jones is quiet and plain from the outside. The only movement on this spring day comes from leaves skittering on the long and winding road that leads to the Tudor-style house.

But inside, the house is vibrating. On this day, as with most, it's from a track by the iconic British band The Beatles.

Jones is an extreme Beatles fan. He's not alone, but few have gone to the length Jones has. Using paint, furnishings, murals and memorabilia, Jones has turned his Lakewood, Wash., home into a temple devoted to The Beatles, classic rock and pop culture.

Jones became a fan of The Beatles at the age of 3 when he heard "A Hard Day's Night." Now 51, he's still just as obsessed. He's been to the birthplace of the Beatles—Liverpool, England—three times.

"Some people go to Jerusalem, I go there," Jones says.

He doesn't dress like the Beatles, he is quick to point out. But he'd be forgiven if he did.

Jones plays keyboard and guitar in a Beatles tribute band, Apple Jam. The name is a nod to The Beatles' recording label. Apple Jam performs songs that were composed but never released by The Beatles. They've put out two albums over eight years and headlined a Beatles festival in 2009.

"I'm not gifted at all," Jones says, strumming an unplugged electric guitar, one of 30 he owns. "I'm a blue-collar musician."

Jones was a longtime employee of Federated Department Stores. "Now I do as little as possible. I push leisure to its limits," he says.

The musician is being a bit coy. The recently completed makeover of his house has been a job all its own.

The first thing a visitor notices, if one makes a right turn upon entering Jones' home, is a recording studio with glassed-in sound booth. A mural of Abbey Road is on one wall of the studio opposite a drum kit. The other walls are apple green and the carpet is black. The numeral 9 is on the door, a nod to the Beatles' "Revolution 9" from "The White Album."

Each of the home's six bedrooms has a different theme. One has sand colored carpet and a large ocean mural. A collection of ukuleles are propped against it. Jones calls it "The Good Vibrations Room" an homage to the Beach Boys.

Another, "The Brit Room," has one wall entirely covered by a Union Jack. The British flag also shows up on the bedspread and light switch cover plates. Jones' master bedroom is done in deep purple with "The love you take is equal to the love you make" stenciled on a wall.

Even the bathrooms get the Beatles treatment. One is done in yellow and aqua colors to the theme of "Yellow Submarine."

When he purchased the house in 2001 it was painted an eggshell white and carpeted with something that might have been seen in a 1980s Reno casino. Jones recently pulled up the last of it. It did come in handy, he notes, during his wild party days. It efficiently camouflaged stains from party guests who couldn't hold their liquor. Today, he lives a quieter life with his Chihuahua, Pixie. The pair dote on each other.

But it wasn't always the two of them.

In September of 2011 he married a woman who he thought would never let him down.

"We were John and Yoko," he recalls.

Jones thought the marriage was going fine until one June day in 2012.

"I came back from a weekend show and she was gone." His wife had left him. He didn't sleep for five months afterward, he says. He didn't have a rubber soul.

But that was yesterday. Today, his home remodel helps to heal his broken heart.

Memorabilia fills the home. Records and autographed pictures of Jimi Hendrix, Jim Morrison and Janis Joplin line the walls.

Local celebrities like TV's "Brakeman Bill" McLain are represented, as is Jimmy "Superfly" Snuka, a professional wrestler who competed at the Tacoma Armory.

Jones started collecting in the 1980s. First it was records, then it became ephemera.

"I was up every weekend driving around the Northwest. I'd come home at night with my car full of stuff," Jones recalls.

Though he quit collecting seven years ago, one room in the house is like Ali Baba's cave—if Mr. Baba had hoarded figurines instead of gold.

Jones calls it "The Toy Room." It's packed with yo-yos, lunch boxes, games and thousands of other items from 20th century pop culture. A sign on the wall reads, "Nothing is real."

"I bought all this stuff in the '80s to sell in the future. Guess what? It's the future."

It's not all "Twist and Shout" in Jones' house. The living room is a calm oasis of white, like a Hollywood version of heaven. It's a tribute to John Lennon's "white period," during which Lennon recorded "Imagine" at his all-white Tittenhurst Park mansion in Ascot. A grand piano, like Lennon's but black, sits in the room. "IMAGINE" is painted on a wall.

Jones still has some work to do on the home. The grand semi-circular staircase will be refinished in black and white to look like piano keys.

That last project will be like others in the house: partly completed by him and partly by others. Or, as Jones puts it, "With a little help from my friends."

∾

[THIRTY-TWO]

How the Beatles Put the Record Center-Stage

By Adam Behr

Adam Behr of Newcastle University analyzes how the Beatles pushed the boundaries of musical expression in popular music through their emphasis on albums. —L.M.

Jef Hanlon spent decades at the forefront of live music promo- tion, putting on acts such as B.B. King, Chuck Berry, Simon and Garfunkel and Stevie Wonder. But were it not for the Beatles, says Hanlon when I interview him:

> *I'd probably now be a retired civil engineer living in a nice part of Lancashire . . . because they opened the door for the northern accents, the northern guys to get down there and do things.*

Hanlon came out of retirement to produce *The Sessions Live*, a "live restaging of the historic recording sessions of the Beatles", which premieres at London's Royal Albert Hall on April 1. The complexity of the show is testament to the changes wrought on the fabric of popular music by the quartet and their production team at Abbey Road.

Hanlon stresses that this isn't a lookalike show with "guys with wigs on their heads and tie-dyed jackets and Cuban-heeled boots". Instead, it is an attempt to capture the *sound* and the recording process. It features 45 performers, including seven singers (veterans of previous Beatles shows) to recreate double-tracked vocals, a six-piece band of leading session musicians and a 21-piece orchestra. It also features actors playing technicians, Yoko Ono, recording engineer Geoff Emerick, and, of course, George Martin, the Beatles' legendary producer.

Spinning records: When Martin died recently, the celebrations of his achievements hinged largely on his status as the "fifth Beatle". But this fruitful relationship was by no means a given in the beginning. Martin, a Guildhall graduate and ex-Royal Navy officer, was a stark contrast to, as Hanlon puts it, the "cheeky scousers who came round from Liverpool and said what they thought".

But Martin's track record of working with the Goons, who were admired by the Beatles, gave him an open ear for innovation and word play. When asked after they worked together if there was anything about the session they didn't like, George Harrison's response — "Well, there's your tie for a start" —broke the ice and led to a revolution in recording history.

For all their success as live performers, the Beatles's ultimate legacy was their recordings. Martin provided the technical and musical ballast for their imaginative flights, from string arrangements, to syncing two four-track machines in different studios, to developing sound effects.

The Beatles pushed the envelope of what popular music *was*, making the studio a creative space—an instrument in itself, rather than just a place to record performances. With George Martin, then, they changed the commercial and artistic realities of popular music, driving forward the recording as the key creative statement and putting the album at the centre of the commercial process. When Martin started at EMI, producers were rule-bound functionaries and engineers, effectively lab assistants in white coats. By the end of the 1960s, the recording studio was at the centre of both creative innovation and social change.

Popular music made a grab for the "authentic" status previously reserved for "high art", just as social barriers had broken down elsewhere when postwar austerity gave way to the more liberal 60s. Again, the Beatles typified this shift, as illustrated by Lennon's exhortation at the Royal Variety Performance: "The people in the cheaper seats, just clap your hands. And the rest of you, if you'll just rattle your jewellery." As Hanlon says, "pop stars two years before the Beatles established themselves wouldn't dream of doing that."

There's no doubt that wider social forces were also at play. But the Beatles's work with Martin and Emerick helped to drive the boat by placing recording at the centre of popular music creativity. Their work helped to define the role of "record production", taking it beyond the technical realm into the creative sphere and making the record, rather than the underlying song, the key text in pop.

Staging recordings: Over 50 years on from their first recording, the extent of that legacy is revealed by the challenges of depicting the process on stage and moving beyond the "tribute show" – not to mention the minefield of rights negotiations involved with anything Beatles-related. (Even former Beatles aren't immune to this, as shown by Paul McCartney's decades-long efforts to reclaim publishing rights to his songs.)

Song suites in the Sessions Live illustrate the changing production process over time, with particular emphasis on tunes featuring groundbreaking techniques. Of this documentary element to the show, Hanlon describes the painstaking attention to detail:

> We've got about 37 different guitars, so that every guitar the Beatles used in the studio will be used on the track it was used on . . . We have the same mics, the same mic positioning from the studio plugs.

That portraying the work of the Beatles, Martin and Emerick requires such effort is a marker of their place in music history. In a way, the Sessions Live crystallises a key change in the dynamic between live performance and recordings driven by the Beatles. Where once the goal was to capture a performance in the studio, the question now is how to recreate the recording on stage. Asked whether he sees this show as a one-off, or a way forward for other such productions, Hanlon laughs: "Well, it's a one-off for me. I'm never working this hard again."

∼

"The Beatles revolutionised music by putting the record centre-stage," Adam Behr. Originally published on The Conversation.

[THIRTY-THREE]

The Post-Beatles Rock Canon

By Dean Biron

The Beatles unleashed a torrent of constant, exponential change onto the rock and roll landscape. Dean Biron lays out how we're still seeing the ripples of the Beatles influence today.—L.M.

∾

Rock 'n' roll is turning 60 . . . about now. The exact date depends on who is doing the reminiscing. But should this event be treated as a birthday celebration or a memorial?

In films such as *Torn Curtain* (1966) and *Frenzy* (1972), Alfred Hitchcock was determined to bring murder to the screen in a way that emphasised the sheer physicality of the act—to show how hard it actually is to kill someone.

It can be just as difficult to kill a concept. In music, the most basic genre distinctions—classical, jazz, rock—stagger on in the 21st century, despite the best efforts of many to render them defunct.

Accounts of rock's demise have been more protracted and painful to observe than one of Hitchcock's elongated death scenes. Yet rock has been defined in so many different ways that the very idea of a definitive start (or end) point seems suspect.

Most orthodox interpretations of the genre betray a kind of bell curve existence. Here the story begins in the mid-1950s, peaks with The Beatles, then undergoes a long descent through punk and beyond. The decline is so widely accepted that it is hard to deny.

The rock canon: Nothing reinforces the waning of rock music more than the rock canon. Every aesthetic form develops narratives of consecration; no other has seen consecration taken to such repetitive extremes.

For decades, listeners have compiled countless lists of rock's greatest albums in barely altered—always male, Anglo-American dominated—arrangements.

The Beatles are immovable at the apex of rock 'n' roll glory, something many music scholars agree with audiences on. The sheer volume of Beatles-related reference texts is astonishing. They range from affectionate anthologies (The 2010 *Cambridge Companion to The Beatles*) to sober examinations (Martin King's 2013 *Men, Masculinity and The Beatles*) to post-1960s doomsday tracts (Elijah Wald's 2009 *How The Beatles Destroyed Rock and Roll*).

Recent debates among nostalgia buffs centre on whether The Beatles' *Revolver* (1966) album has overtaken *Sgt. Pepper's Lonely Hearts Club Band* (1967), long considered the genre's foremost artefact. For their 2013 book *100 Best Albums of All Time*, Australian authors Toby Creswell and Craig Mathieson claim some kind of subversive coup by rejecting *Sgt. Pepper's* in favour of its predecessor.

The Beatles dance with Stockhausen: Yet what The Beatles also evoke is rock's disintegration as a clear-cut style. Reductive takes on their legacy contrast with the innovative nature of their music. The 1967 cover of *Sgt. Pepper's* gives a major clue here.

Peering out morosely from the back row of that famous celebrity gathering is German composer Karlheinz Stockhausen, whose pioneering *Hymnen* (Anthems) appeared the same year. A melange of dismembered national anthems for tape, electronics and/or orchestra,

Hymnen suggests contradictions and cross-fertilisations; it speaks of sonic borders being torn down.

The following year, The Beatles were channelling Stockhausen with Revolution 9 from their White Album.

At the time, in an interview with the *New Musical Express*, Paul McCartney expressed admiration for Stockhausen and fellow modern composer Luciano Berio, saying he was "sick of doing sounds that people can claim to have heard before".

The Beatles were always looking ahead, so it is ironic that their high points are now frozen in time as insurmountable monuments.

One contemporary artist who embraced the mixing of musical categories was English film director Nicolas Roeg. The soundtrack to *Walkabout* (1971), his key contribution to the new Australian cinema, combined excerpts from Hymnen with an opulent John Barry score and the Rod Stewart song "Gasoline Alley."

Unfortunately, the subsequent rock canon incorporates diversity only in perverse ways. For instance, Creswell and Mathieson, like many before them, inexplicably claim Miles Davis's *Kind of Blue* (1959) as a rock touchstone (supposedly jazz's great gift to the form, despite Davis, under the influence of Stockhausen and Jimi Hendrix, releasing a wealth of memorable rock-tinged recordings in the 1970s).

Meanwhile, inventive new artists are largely shunted out to the margins, ushered there by ageing baby-boomers who long ago pronounced the landscape of rock music to be "thoroughly explored".

A 'delta of microcultures': Rock has now devolved into what British writer Simon Reynolds terms "a delta of microcultures", each itself fragmenting at frightening speed—from metal to rap to alt-country, from drone to new folk to dub-step.

Narrow, sentimentalised versions of classic rock history banish these new developments to a "not-rock" wilderness, helping ensure the mummification of the form.

While there is much fine rock-inflected music being made today, including by Australians, the contradiction remains that deeply nostalgic celebrations of rock only serve to strangle it as a living form.

As long as the acclaim is mostly for what was, not what might come next, the extended death throes of rock will likely continue to play out well past its 60th anniversary.

～

"The Beatles ruled rock 'n' roll—but it's time to let it be," Dean Biron. Originally published on The Conversation.

[THIRTY-FOUR]

Going Mono a Mano with the Beatles

By Mark Caro

The Beatles experience has much to do with the sweeping, complex soundscapes they create. That goes hand-in-hand with stereo. Can you really enjoy the Beatles in mono? Yes, according to the Chicago Tribune's Marco Caro. —L.M.

∼

The pin-your-ears-back moment came on a song I'd heard thousands of times.

Having read of John Lennon's complaint about the stereo mix of "Revolution" ("They took a heavy record and turned it into a piece of ice cream"), I decided to do an A-B comparison. First up was the stereo version from the *Past Masters* double disc of the Beatles stereo vinyl boxed set issued two years ago.

The rat-a-tat electric guitar started it off, Ringo Starr's drums came in with a bang, and T.J. Shanoff —a Second City director/writer/music director and an even more rabid Beatles geek than me—and

I bobbed our heads as we listened on very high-end equipment at Audio Consultants in Evanston. This sure didn't sound like ice cream.

Then I put on the "Revolution" from the triple-disc *Mono Masters* record inside the new *The Beatles in Mono* vinyl boxed set. The heavily distorted guitars exploded out of the speakers like a nuclear blast, Ringo's drum crack and Lennon's scream tore through the din, and as the rest of the arrangement snarled in, I found myself feeling like that guy in the old Maxell ads with his hair blown back by the sound.

"Holy (moly)!" I exclaimed.

I knew this song so well, yet I'd never heard it so nasty. What was the difference?

Three factors are involved.

The mix: The Beatles and producer George Martin created distinct mixes of instruments, vocals and sound effects for records that came out in mono, the single-channel format prevalent through the mid-to-late 1960s, and in stereo, which spread the sound over two speakers and is the way modern listeners are most used to hearing these and most other songs. Because of mono's dominance through 1967's landmark album *Sgt. Pepper's Lonely Hearts Club Band*, the Beatles are said to have spent more time on those mixes than the stereo ones.

The Beatles (aka 1968's the White Album) was the last Beatles album issued in mono, though in the U.S. only the stereo version was available. Singles, including "Hey Jude"/"Revolution" (1968), were issued in mono, all the better to hear blasting out of a car radio, so those mixes often were punchier.

Vinyl: *The Beatles in Mono* came out on CD in 2009 at the same time that the stereo albums were given a CD upgrade for the first time since 1987. So this mono "Revolution" had been available for a while, yet I'd never felt the difference between it and the stereo one as I did when I heard the song on mono vinyl.

The audiophile crowd argues that vinyl, which uses an analog process to embed the sound waves into a record's grooves, is a fuller, more accurate, warmer representation of music than CDs and other formats that convert sound into digital files. Although vinyl isn't nearly as popular as in the pre-CD days, its continued resurgence in this MP3/earbud era speaks to a growing appreciation of its sonic qualities.

The transfer: The 2009 stereo and mono CDs used updated technology to create new digital remasters from the original master recordings. The records in the 2012 stereo vinyl box were made from these same remasters, meaning the process essentially moved from analog to digital to analog. Some of the criticism of that boxed set stemmed from the perceived sonic compromises inherent in the digital conversion.

Instead of using the same procedures for the mono vinyl box—that is, transfer the 2009 CD versions back to LP—the reissue engineers opted to return to the original tapes to create a new cutting master for each album. The process, in other words, remained analog the entire time, with these records, like the stereo ones, being pressed on premium 180-gram vinyl.

This bypassing of the digital world has a good number of sound aficionados praising the new mono box as the ultimate Beatles audiophile collection, though it doesn't contain such stereo-only albums as *Abbey Road* and *Let it Be.*

Of course, there's a reason we listen primarily to stereo these days. It provides a more spatially rich experience, enabling you to hear individual instruments more distinctly as they're spread over the acoustical equivalent of a wide screen.

If you're listening to "A Day in the Life" on headphones, the stereo version will make your head swirl in a way that the mono one won't. But there's also an undeniable immediacy and intensity to the new mono vinyl version, as well as unexpected levels of color and dimension. Upon hearing the new mono "A Day in the Life," Shanoff said this was the first time he'd truly felt the song's "nightmare" quality.

The attraction of the early Beatles mono recordings, particularly the rockers, is more basic: They come straight at you, in contrast to the pronounced separation of the primitive stereo efforts.

So should you buy the new mono vinyl box?

That depends on whether:

- You have about $375 to plunk down for the 11 albums spread over 14 discs plus a handsome photo-filled, coffee-table-style book that elaborates on the albums' history and technological aspects.
- You own a turntable.
- You like the Beatles. (If you don't, thanks for reading this far anyway.)
- You already own the stereo albums on CD or vinyl or the mono albums on CD or the originally issued records. If you have pristine copies of all of the Beatles' original mono albums, good for you—but that probably means you're enough of a fan to buy the new box anyway. If you're more of a casual listener, you may feel that owning the music once is enough no matter the perceived quality upgrade.
- You have more of a pick-and-choose than completionist mentality. The individual LPs are available separately (single albums run for about $20, the double White Album for about $35, the triple *Mono Masters* for about $60), so you're free to decide how to augment your collection—and buying all of the albums individually is still cheaper than getting the box.

If you're happy with your stereo version of *Help!* do you need the mono one? The mono *Help!*—both on CD and vinyl—is notably muddier than the brighter stereo mixes. (Geeky but unavoidable note: The stereo versions on the recent CD and vinyl releases of *Help!* and *Rubber Soul* are Martin's 1987 remixes in which he recalibrated the originals' extreme left-right separation. Yet the mono CDs of those two albums also include the lopsided early stereo versions as a sort of 2-for-1 deal.) The "Help!" title track features a different Lennon lead vocal from the stereo and is missing the familiar tambourine that pushes the song forward. Is it superior? No. Is it different? Yes.

The superior/different distinction is most pronounced on the White Album. Listening to it in mono after a lifetime of living with the stereo version is a disorienting experience: The album's opening jet-and-shout intro to "Back in the U.S.S.R." is altered; "Blackbird" and "Piggies" feature alternate bird chirps and hog grunts, respectively, that appear at unfamiliar points; Ringo's "Don't Pass Me By" plays at a faster speed and has a different fiddle coda; Paul McCartney's sung bass line of "I Will" doesn't kick in until after the first verse; and "Helter Skelter" is missing its final fade-in, including Ringo's cry of "I've got blisters on my fingers!" (A regrettable omission.)

Given that stereo technology was pretty far along by the time *The Beatles* was recorded, it's tough to make the case that the mono version is preferable. Yet if you know that album inside and out, there's something cool about hearing a version that's fresh to your ears—and the transition from the delicate "Mother Nature's Son" to the raucous "Everybody's Got Something to Hide Except Me and My Monkey" has never sounded so dramatic.

Which mono versions actually are superior?

The first albums, *Please Please Me* and *With the Beatles*, and the early rock singles hit you right between the eyes in mono, especially in these new vinyl versions. As stereo recording and mixing improved on subsequent records, there's more gray area.

On the new vinyl mono of *Rubber Soul*, the bass on "Norwegian Wood (This Bird Has Flown)" is more rounded and distinct than ever, even if the acoustic guitar and sitar may be crisper in stereo. Give the new mono *Revolver* a spin, and you'll notice not only how the birdish sound effects of "Tomorrow Never Knows" swoop in and out more jarringly than on the stereo version but also how much more present and intimate McCartney's voice sounds on "Eleanor Rigby."

As for which mono LP you should get no matter which other versions you may own, that's easy: *Sgt. Pepper's Lonely Hearts Club Band*. The mix includes many differences that also qualify as improvements: the trippy phasing effects on Lennon's "Lucy in the Sky With Diamonds" vocals, the correct-speed (i.e. not slowed down) "She's Leaving Home," the punched-up energy and extra crowd noises of the title track's reprise, with a smoother transition into "A Day in the Life." The overall listening experience will explode any preconceptions you have about mono offering a small, boxy sound.

I realize this is all very annoying: Here are yet more spiffed-up recordings that we're expected to buy from a defunct-for-44-years-and-counting band. When does it all end?

In truth, the Beatles were slow to upgrade their catalog and have been playing catch-up for years. The rub is with these new editions having been staggered over the past several years, they come across as an annual grab for the holiday gift market, which, of course, they are.

But from a pure sound standpoint, I'm more knocked out and surprised by these mono vinyl records than any of the other recent reissues—and I've been listening on my own home stereo with a relatively ancient, not expensive turntable. When you've heard these songs so many times, you don't think more revelations await you. I was happy to be wrong.

Still, if the Beatles' reps announce that they'll next be reissuing all of the stereo vinyl albums in pure analog transfers, then I'll be annoyed. Though come to think of it . . .

~

[THIRTY-FIVE]

A Dentist's Quest to Clone John Lennon

By Grant Burningham

We all miss John. But some people—including this dentist—won't move on. Who knows? Maybe he'll be successful and we'll have John 2.0 recording "Revolution #10" sometime soon. —L.M.

~

There is a dentist in Canada who is trying to clone John Lennon. It sounds complicated and fantastical, and maybe it is, but it is also that simple, if you pare it down to its essence: a dentist, a molar that is said to have come from the Beatle's mouth and a long-term plot—10, 20, however many years it takes—to produce a clone.

There are obstacles. For one, human cloning is legally prohibited in Canada. It is also not yet a scientific reality, though experts say it's probably biologically possible, or will be soon enough. Those facts don't perturb Dr. Michael Zuk, the dentist in question. "This is obviously science fiction at this point, but technology's moving in that direction," Zuk recently told *Newsweek*. "My prediction would be five years."

After he gave an interview on the U.K.'s Channel 4 in April, Zuk became the subject of massive online media coverage, but since then he has laid low and clarified little about his ambitious plans.

So I reached out, using an email introduction I wish I had the privilege of using every day: "Hi, Dr. Zuk, I'm a reporter for *Newsweek*, and I'm intrigued by your apparent plans to clone John Lennon."

His reply was prompt: It came later that night, while he was "working the night shift." But he rarely talks to the media, he explained. "Trying not to do many interviews about the story as we (me & the tooth) have a person in LA working on a documentary dedicated to human cloning, ethics, science and legal issues," he wrote. "It all sounds crazy so I'm laying low."

I read it twice. He had used the pronoun "we" to refer to himself and a molar once in the mouth of a rock star who has been dead for 33 years. I kept pressing. He agreed to "buzz" me soon. Turns out, he wanted to clear up some misconceptions in the media.

We spoke for 30 minutes and 50 seconds the following week.

I asked—of course—how he had acquired this rare treasure. In November 2011, he explained, he spotted it online at Omega Auctions, a U.K. auction house, and thought, "Jesus, this is my big break!" So he outbid the American bidder seeking the same item and, 19,500 pounds (or just over $31,000) later, became the privileged owner of a tiny piece of John Lennon's DNA. That's not a modest chunk of cash, but Zuk had recently sold a dental clinic and written a book, *Confession of a Former Cosmetics Dentist*.

"I just knew that the tooth still had so many different avenues to be explored, including the scientific side and maybe science fiction writing," he told me, speaking in a distinctly Canadian accent. "So I'm definitely milking the tooth for all that it's worth, I guess you could say, right?"

Zuk confirmed the veracity of the molar because it had come directly from Lennon's housekeeper, who signed documents from a lawyer and included son Julian Lennon's tooth. "It comes with very legitimate paperwork and all that kind of thing," he said.

This is not his only adventure with dead celebrities. He owns bits of Elvis Presley's hair, models of Presley's mouth and "one little strand" of Jimi Hendrix's hair. Once, he was offered Shaquille O'Neal's tooth.

But this is the first time he has taken an interest in using such an item in the service of an altogether more ambitious project: human cloning. From watching news and TV shows about cloning, Zuk learned that teeth are often used as DNA evidence. He hatched the idea while chatting and joking around with a former employee, a woman who offered to be the surrogate mother: "You'd take the DNA, you'd insert it into a cell, then you'd stimulate the cell to reproduce, then you'd insert it into a woman's uterus to be the host. So it's kind of almost like artificial insemination."

But he is not sure she should be the one to take on that role. "I think there'd be thousands of people who'd realize it would be an opportunity of a lifetime," he said. So, I ask: How will the project move forward?

The plan is to find a company that will participate in a documentary exploring "DNA sequencing and the legal and ethical issues," Zuk told me. He added that he has a representative in Hollywood trying to drum up interest in this project, though he was vague on the specifics of the potential film. "There's a lot of time to think these things through, and if it doesn't work out, it certainly will be something that will be opened up in the future. You can imagine that someone like the dictator of North Korea might start popping up replicas of himself to try to perpetuate his insanity."

That brings up another issue: ethical concerns. Cloning is, by definition, bringing a human being into the world. Zuk acknowledged the dangers to the clone himself: kidnapping, extortion, drug habits.

"I'm conflicted, of course," Zuk said. "It's not something I would just participate in without thinking it all the way through." He compared it to the handling of a child star. "It's a human being, and who is going to be the family and who's going to be the responsible one that oversees the whole business side of it? It'd be a whole new realm of entertainment law, I'm guessing."

It has been reported that Zuk wishes to raise the young Beatle clone as his son, offering up guitar lessons and other fatherly services. This is untrue.

"I'm not going to be the daddy," he said. "I don't think I would want that responsibility, a parent of one of the most famous clones in the world. I would look at the whole process as if he is part of the family, but not necessarily be the father." Nor would he want the media harassment that would come with being the handler of a child containing the DNA that wrote "A Day in the Life."

Still, he wishes to remain in control of the cloning process, if in fact it takes place. "I think I would probably have a little more ethical considerations than an average company which would be more enthused about their own publicity."

None of it will happen if Yoko Ono gets her way, however. The Beatle widow's lawyer has sent Zuk a letter asking him to abandon his plans. It was "little bit on the threatening side," Zuk said. Defending his right to do what he wishes with the tooth, Zuk directed me to the story of Henrietta Lacks, whose Wikipedia page he has studied in depth. Lacks was the Virginia woman whose cells were cultured by a German-American scientist and became the first human immortal cell line to be used in scientific research. Lacks' family objected to their use, but in 1990 the Supreme Court ruled that a human's discarded tissue and cells are not that person's personal property.

Zuk emailed me with further information on Lacks' case. "Should Yoko get special treatment over a poor black woman's family from the experiments of the 1950s?" he wondered. "I will not sell the DNA rights for any price without having controlling interest in the strategic decisions which ensure the same safety that any newborn would have."

Then he sent me a link to an article claiming that Sean Lennon, the Beatle's only child with Ono, is "furious and fed up" with the cloning efforts, as well as a mock-up of a flier for a potential science fiction film about the process. Zuk said he's looking for a screenwriter for the proposed movie and wondered if I'd be interested in the job. I'm still considering the offer.

[THIRTY-SIX]

Paul Reflects on Yesterday, Today, and Tomorrow

By Hillel Italie

As Paul aged, he seems to have come to terms with his past. He no longer stays away from Beatles songs at concerts, but plays them proudly—including tunes penned by deceased bandmates John and George. Whereas in the past, Paul could not help seeing the Beatles story through the lens of his own often-complicated life experiences, he now takes a step back and contemplates the historic, cultural significance of the band he helped create—as he expresses in this piece. —L.M.

∾

Sir Paul McCartney is 72, and only the wrinkles give his years away. Interviewed recently at his midtown Manhattan office suite, he seems as boyish and light-footed as he was on stage decades ago for *The Ed Sullivan Show*, his manner informal, his build slender and well suited for jeans and a form-fitting sweater. He's so young in his thoughts that he will dismiss the idea of a memoir as a project for his 70s, catch himself, and dismiss a book again as if time were still a distant brother.

Memories can be found in his otherwise bright and modern office, from a small black and white photo taken of him by his late wife, Linda, to the abstract paintings by his late friend Willem de Kooning. But he is here to promote the present, a score he completed for *Destiny*, a first-person shooter game for PlayStation and Xbox. The premise was intriguing partly because he is no more adept at video games than he is at reading sheet music (many rock stars can't), and because the closing song he wrote, the ballad "Hope for the Future," captures how he looks upon the world.

"I thought, 'Seeing it's a shoot-em-up game, I will be the optimistic hope for the future,'" he says. "I will write something that sums up that side of the game."

Writing songs on commission has been a pastime for McCartney since his years with the Beatles, when he composed the soundtrack for the 1966 film *The Family Way*. He likes the challenge of fitting a piece of music into a pre-existing narrative, comparing it to solving a crossword puzzle. One of his favorite tests was coming up with the theme song, a top five solo hit for McCartney, for the 1973 James Bond thriller *Live and Let Die*.

"It's like 'Live and Let Die,' how the hell am I am going to write a song like that?" he says. "I can't change the title. I can't say I'm going to write a song, 'Live and Let Fish.' Then you sit around and go, 'OK, "You used to say 'Live and let live' . . . '" You work out a whole hypothesis."

McCartney doesn't think of himself as a personal writer in the tradition of his former collaborator, John Lennon. His songs often are less about his own life than about assuming a mood or identity. So he is as comfortable declaring "Hope for the Future" as he was confiding "I believe in yesterday," as likely to imagine a lonely old woman ("Eleanor Rigby") as to put in a word for "Silly Love Songs." At times he takes on social causes, or at least tries. Having written "Blackbird" for the civil rights movement in the '60s, he attempted a song about police killings in Ferguson, Missouri, and New York City.

"I was thinking recently about all these protests in New York and around the country. I thought it would be great to put something down about that, just to add my voice to the thousands of people walking in the streets," he says. "I thought it through and it just didn't come easily. I'm not giving up on it, but it didn't come easily, whereas some other emotions might come easily to me."

While forever a Beatle in the hearts of millions, he keeps his mind open to all moments. He sends out tweets on occasion and texts his friends, although the fine points of Spotify are beyond him (that's what lawyers are for). Sam Smith is a favorite young singer, and McCartney recently attended a Jay-Z/Kanye West concert, found it "amazing" and praised their lyrics as "modern poetry."

McCartney makes frequent visits to his native Liverpool, where he helped found The Liverpool Institute for Performing Arts on the site of the school he and George Harrison attended as boys. And he keeps in close touch with family members and past associates, enjoying local gossip or joking with Beatles producer Sir George Martin. Loved ones speak to him from beyond. McCartney finds himself remembering his late father's pet expressions, like "Get stripped, you're on next," meaning asking a guest to take his coat off. While working on a song—the melodies come to him constantly—he might summon the spirit of Lennon.

"I imagine myself back into a room with John, and I'll think (about a lyric), 'Ugh, that's no good.' And I'll imagine him saying, 'No, can't do that.' So I'm using him as a sort of judge of what I'm doing," McCartney says.

History—the Beatles, England, childhood—follows him everywhere, whether to a White House party where young friends of the Obamas gushed like the kids of old, or a birthday party in Tokyo for his current wife, Nancy. The entertainment was Queen and Beatles tribute bands.

"I had a kind of very emotional moment when we were sitting there—it could have been the alcohol," he says. "And I'm thinking, 'My God.' The power of British music finally came home to me. All the way across the world, in Japan, these guys were breaking down

Queen songs, and the others Beatles songs. They were replicating them amazingly. They got all the orchestra parts on 'I Am the Walrus.' They may not even speak the language that well, but they speak these songs beautifully.

"I should know that we've had that effect, because it's historically true. But it doesn't always come home to you in quite the way it did that night. I was welling up and I was (thinking) 'I can't well up to a Queen tribute band.'"

~

"McCartney reflects on yesterday, today and tomorrow," Hillel Italie. Licensed from The Washington Times. © Associated Press. All Rights Reserved. iCopyright license: 3.7280-43762.

[About FanReads]

Founded in 2016, FanReads publishes collections of the greatest stories ever told for fans of sports, screen, music and gaming.

Visit www.fanreads.com to sign up for FanReader, our free weekly digest of the very best writing about sports, screen, music and gaming delivered straight to your inbox each Monday.

Follow us on Facebook and Twitter for news and special offers.

www.fanreads.com

Twitter: @FanReads

Facebook: FanReads

info@fanreads.com

[More From FanReads]

Sports

Fighting Words: The Greatest Muhammad Ali Stories Ever Told

Bat Flip: The Greatest Toronto Blue Jays Stories Ever Told

Screen

For the Watch: The Greatest Game of Thrones Stories Ever Told

Games

Catch 'Em All: The Greatest Pokémon Go Stories Ever Told

www.fanreads.com

[Join the FanReads Team]

Curators

FanReads is looking for editors to curate fan-based anthologies. If you're a skilled writer / editor, a motivated entrepreneur and a fan of sports, screen or music, we want to hear from you.

Reach out to submissions@fanreads.com with your credentials and potential topics of interest.

Contributors

FanReads is always on the lookout for the very best writing on fan-based themes.

If you've published great content on sports, screen or music and want us to consider your content for republication in a FanReads title, please let us know at submissions@fanreads.com.

submissions@fanreads.com

[About the Editor]

Luis Miguel is a writer, marketer, and business owner. In addition to the Beatles, he enjoys listening to artists including Genesis, Mike Oldfield and Brian Eno.

He runs Ket-Go Digital Media and lives in Fort Lauderdale, Florida with his wife and children.

Made in the USA
Monee, IL
16 December 2019